Ain't Misbehavin'

A Good Behaviour Guide for Family Dogs

BY

David Appleby

ILLUSTRATIONS BY

Andrew Marland

Broadcast
BOOKS

Why we want dogs to live with us

First published 1997

by Broadcast Books
4 Cotham Vale
Bristol BS6 6HR

8th printing 2002

A copy of the CIP entry for this book is available from the British Library.

ISBN: 1874092 7 29

Design by Ed Crewe

Printed in Great Britain by The Bath Press, Bath

To Pauline, James and Richard whom I love very much.

About the Author

David Appleby specialises in the field of pet behaviour counselling, and in this role advises pet owners, on referral from their vets, who are experiencing problems with their pet. David is a member of the Association of Pet behaviour Counsellors and holds a post-graduate diploma in Companion Animal Counselling. He is also a former RAF dog handler, and former Guide Dogs for the Blind instructor. He runs regular clinics at the Queen's Veterinary School, Cambridge University and at the Pet Behaviour Centre in Worcestershire, as well as clinics in Derby, Nottingham, Leicester, Northampton and Birmingham.

David is a regular contributor to pet magazines, and is the author and publisher of a series of popular booklets on dog and cat behaviour sold through veterinary practices nationwide.

Contents

Acknowledgements

Some of the contents of this book I have previously had published in *Dogs Today* magazine. I would like to thank the editor, Beverly Cuddy, for kindly agreeing to its use.

Thanks also go to fellow members of the Association of Pet Behaviour Counsellors without whose free exchange of ideas some of this book would not have seen the light of day. An especial thanks to APBC members Dr Anne McBride for her thoughts on *"Off Training"* and Val Strong for allowing me to print her diet rationale. I would also like to thank Elizabeth Kershaw and Nina Bondarenko for their input on *"Clicker Training"*. Where appropriate I have indicated references for academic work.

My thanks must also go to those people who suffered the first drafts of **"Ain't Misbehaving"** and their useful feedback. These include my publisher, Catherine Mason, whom I must also thank for her belief in this book, her patience and editorial skills.

Finally I must thank my clients and their dogs whose experiences inspired me to write this book and all those people whose ideas have been absorbed into the way we approach living with our dogs.

Foreword

Canine behaviour problems are very common, but in the main the dogs that display them ain't misbehaving - they are just misunderstood. Most problems are the result of normal behaviour in inappropriate circumstances and the way to prevent or resolve them is to understand both why they occur, and the dog's perception of what is going on.

After receiving help from a pet behaviour counsellor, many owners will make comments like "it seems so obvious when it is pointed out!". The control of most pet problems lies well within the capabilities of the owner, either acting alone or with the guidance of a pet behaviour counsellor. The purpose of this book is to point out the information necessary for owners of all dogs to understand how to **prevent** and **cure** many of the most common problems.

You will find that this book does not have a list of troublesome behaviours and a matching list of recipes for resolving them. Providing such a list of procedures would encourage the reader to try and suppress the symptoms of a problem without addressing the cause. This would not only be inefficient; it could also result in the problem behaviour getting worse, or being manifested in another form. Many factors can contribute to the development of behaviour problems and this book will help you identify and address these in the most appropriate manner.

In most cases you will find that implementing the suggestions given in this book will not involve time taken out of your normal daily routine, just an alteration of what you do when the problem behaviours occur. Where extra time has to be set aside the medium and long-term benefit is that you will no longer have to lose time fruitlessly trying to stop or control an unwanted pattern of behaviour.

Although this book provides an insight into how your dog's behaviour problems can be addressed, please remember it is mainly intended as a guide. If your dog has a severe problem, if you are unsure of the right approach or if the problem continues to occur, you should refer to the Further Help section for professional guidance. Under any circumstances you must avoid putting yourself or other people at risk.

If, after reading this book, you do decide that you need professional help from a pet behaviour counsellor you will already have an understanding of the approach that will be involved and the background knowledge necessary will already be in place. You will also be in a position to know how to prevent the problem from getting any worse before you get help.

In this book I have made reference to experimental work with rats, dogs and performing dolphins. This work has allowed us to amass a store of useful knowledge, but how I feel about these experiments and captive animals used for performing is another matter.

Introduction

Canine and human societies are so similar that we fit together like hand in glove. Man works co-operatively with other members of his group, and this co-operation enabled our ancestors to hunt animals that were larger or faster than themselves, while communal living provided benefits such as defence and support in rearing the young. Stability within the group was maintained by a hierarchical structure characterised by a complex mix of relationships.

Although in the developed world man has moved away from his original role as hunter, family life has continued with the same underlying structures, and dogs are able to find, in our society, a substitute for the packs in which they evolved. Like man, the dog is also a co-operative hunter, shares the defence of territory and raises its young communally. The harmony of the pack is maintained through a complex social structure based on dominance and submission. Of course, the domestic dog has changed and it is not quite the pack animal its wild cousins are. Nonetheless its relationship with man is based on the similarity between family and pack and, as we shall see, the process of the domestic dog's integration into human family life is made possible by the effects of early socialisation with other animals.

Our view of our relationship with dogs, and our understanding of the appropriate way to interact with and train them, has been distorted. The contemporary portrayal of dogs in books, films and cartoons, as T.V. heroes, in media hypes together with a general change in society's needs have encouraged us to treat dogs as if they are little human beings. Generally they are expected to just fit in with us. All too frequently, when things don't work out because the dog develops a behaviour problem or does not do well in training, we blame the dog rather than ourselves. But most dogs that display a behaviour problem or don't do well at training are not rogue dogs. They are victims of a system where either:

- the dog's owner is unaware of their dog's perspective regarding its relationship with man,
- the owner uses inefficient approaches to rearing and training,
- or both.

However this does not mean we should perpetuate the horrid and inappropriate maxim "there are no bad dogs, just bad owners". All the owners I meet as a pet behaviour counsellor are kind and caring. They are often dismayed when they find that, despite having done everything they thought was right, their relationship with their dog has run into difficulties. Often the cause is a lack of the right information, and therefore the use of inappropriate approaches is perpetuated. Many dogs do not develop serious problems despite their owner's inappropriate attempts to control them, and this tends to lull us all into a false sense of security. But every now and then things go badly wrong.

- In Canada, the major cause of death in dogs under two years of age is euthanasia for behaviour problems.[1]
- The Blue Cross (one of the U.K.'s rescue societies) conducted a survey which revealed that 32% of the owners who were giving up their dogs gave 'a behaviour problem' as the reason.[2]
- Dr Valerie O'Farrell at Edinburgh University found that of the owners she surveyed, [3] one in five reported that their dog had a serious behaviour problem, three out of five reported nuisance behaviour, and only one in five said they had no problem at all. In this book I hope to show the reader what the warning signs might be, long before they can develop into anything more serious.

How can we avoid behaviour and training problems? Happily the answer is simple. We must view our relationships with our dogs from their perspective, and regard interaction and training in an appropriate manner as the way to develop and maintain good behaviour. This book is designed to help you by showing:

- how worst case scenarios can develop
- how to cure problems
- and most importantly, how to prevent them.

You will find that you will be provided with a range of possible approaches to many of the problems discussed. This does not mean that you have to get bogged down in what you should or should not be doing to the point where it spoils the spontaneity of the relationship you have with your dog! Just keep a sense of proportion based on the information you find in the rest of these pages.

NOTES

1. Professor Don McKewan, DUM Dept. of Population Medicine, Ontario Veterinary College, Ontario, Canada.

2. Bailey.G. *Parting With a Pet Survey* (Blue Cross 1991)

3. O'Farrell, V. *Manual of Canine Behaviour (2nd Edition)* British Small Animal Veterinary Association, (Cheltenham 1992)

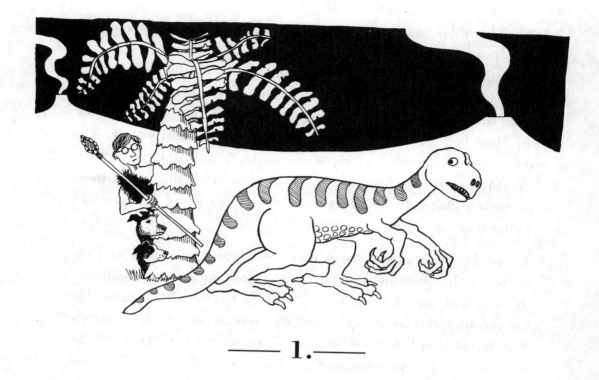

— 1. —

Man and Dog: An Old Partnership

No-one knows for sure how the dog's relationship with man began. Maybe wolves followed our ancestors' nomadic wanderings, staying close to their encampments so that they could scavenge. Their loitering presence became a useful early warning system if predators or rival groups were in the vicinity, so their presence was encouraged, and then gradually incorporated into man's hunting and domestic life.[1] There was also the added bonus that if times were hard they could be eaten, as indeed dogs still are in some parts of the world.

A recent theory [2] suggests that the process of domestication started when man changed from hunter-gatherer to farmer.

13

Wherever there was a small farming community there would also be that most valuable of resources, the rubbish tip. Such a rare opportunity to find food with little effort attracted the wolves, and those less inclined to run off than the rest of the pack when people were close by got the best pickings. As a result they were healthier and had better breeding success than the more timid wolves. The domestic dog evolved as these increasingly man-tolerant wolves interbred over many generations, and man gradually tamed these animals sufficiently for them to be trusted to guard his livestock rather than eat it.

Archaeological evidence shows that even earliest man and wolf co-existed in the same areas, sometimes in close proximity [3], although the wolf had not yet been 'tamed'. Recent DNA studies suggest that the genetic variation from the wolf that was to become the domestic dog started long before the process of domestication.[4] However the remains of what we recognise as dogs rather than tamed wolves around human settlements date from only about **12,000** years ago. The remains of dogs dating from two to three thousand years later are found in significant numbers, and this time scale matches the development of farming communities. What is clear is that once dog-like animals started to appear, they did so simultaneously in many regions of the world.

The shape we recognise as dog rather than wolf developed because the genes passed on by wolves, or a variant of wolves able to tolerate the presence of man, coincided with immaturity. Along with a readiness to tolerate man, these early wolf-dogs inherited a genetic resistance to growing up. Man accelerated the process by favouring the most friendly and cooperative animals, with the most puppyish, least lupine appearance. This is called **neotenisation**. In other words, the dogs that evolved were permanently immature versions of their wild cousins.

What caused the variation in the appearance and behaviour of the different breeds? In the first four months of life wolf cubs go though identifiable stages during which their repertoire of hunting behaviour develops. It has been suggested that different types of dog developed from these different stages; and that they are permanently at that point of development whatever their size happens to be. (5) These stages are:

1. Mostly play behaviour

The behaviour of the breeds that developed from the first stage of development can be analysed as being **10%** hunting and **90%** play. This group includes the modern St Bernard and Maremma. The Maremma is famed for being gentle with sheep; after socialisation with a flock at the puppy stage it will treat sheep as its own kind, and guard them without displaying predatory behaviour towards them.

2. Learning to explore and carry things by mouth

The next stage of development has given rise to **Object Players**; dogs for whom object investigation by mouth and carrying is very important. Among this group are the various types of Retriever.

3. Learning to stalk things and head them off

The third group has resulted in the **Development Headers** (heading off the prey) and **Stalkers**. This group includes the Collies, which show an incomplete repertoire of predatory behaviour because they tend to stalk and chase but are not so inclined to go in for the kill as the fourth group.

4. Learning to hold and immobilise prey

The fourth group are more inclined to try and grab hold of an animal they are chasing and have a behaviour repertoire that is

15

about **90%** predatory and only **10%** play. This group includes breeds such as Huskies.

As man's needs changed and the tasks he had to perform became increasingly specialised, he matched the skills shown by different types of dogs to the tasks he needed them for. Although early men were selective, they did not deliberately set out to create new patterns of behaviour in dogs of different design. By favouring those individuals with the most aptitude for a particular task, and discarding the rest, the desired characteristics became more pronounced. Consequently all breeds have the range of behaviours they inherited from the wolf, but the capacity to perform particular tasks has been increased in some and allowed to diminish in others.

This specialisation brought with it a change in appearance: Greyhounds provide a good example of how these changes took place. Dogs that particularly liked to chase were favoured by men who needed dogs to chase prey for them. The faster they could run the better, so man favoured the faster runners from this group by keeping the puppies bred from them. The result was a long legged dog capable of high speed that required very little stimulation to encourage it to chase other animals. With the development of greyhound racing as a sport, the breed was standardised into the remarkably streamlined creatures that we know today.

Early man had developed a number of breeds, although the range was small and they were still, in the main, dogs of a type; hunters by scent or by sight, guard dogs, fighting and war dogs. It was not until Roman times that specific breeds ranging from large hunting dogs to lap dogs became established. The modern notion of defining a breed by precise criteria of size, shape, colour, etc., only began in the nineteenth century. In an urban environment when dogs were no longer needed solely for useful work, selection began to be made on cosmetic rather than functional grounds. A proliferation of 'breed standards' developed as a result of the emergence of competitive dog showing. As a result, some of the differences between the breeds became grotesquely exaggerated.

Why do we keep dogs now?

The main reason we keep pets now is for companionship. The practice of keeping dogs as companions has been with us since ancient times; but it has become more common and less the preserve of the rich[6]. Although some dogs are still kept for their working abilities, most live in our homes providing support for our emotional rather than our practical needs.

What people get out of the relationship is very varied. Dogs can provide a sense of security, companionship, affection and constancy that may not be readily available in the outside world. Sometimes the bond between dog and owner is so close that its death causes as much grieving as the loss of a family member. Dog ownership normally reduces stress, encourages exercise and, in a modern society where people are more than ever isolated from each other, the presence of a dog helps owners initiate dialogue with strangers.[7] All in all, dogs are important in our lives.

Horses for courses

People often ask about the intelligence of different breeds of dog and compare one with another. A television company once picked up on a story of this nature and asked if a recent report that stated the Afghan Hound is the most stupid breed was true. No doubt it seemed like a good wheeze that would fill a slot on day-time television - but their enthusiasm was misplaced. The Afghan Hound may not do very much, but what it does do it does very well. As a hunter, it is a veritable Exocet on legs, its eyes locking onto the moving target it will pursue until it has run it down or become exhausted in the attempt. Admittedly, it is not as good at the task as a Greyhound, but the Greyhound would not last long in Afghanistan's mountainous terrain with a coat that is the canine equivalent of a T shirt!

None the less a dog's apparent intelligence and responsiveness to training rouses more than idle curiosity in most owners. The Border Collie is an example of this. Its sleek lines, good road holding, acceleration and above all its responsiveness to the handler's slightest whim make it the model which most obedience and agility competitors either own, or use as a benchmark against which other breeds are compared. The Border Collie is also a good retriever, but it is not a breed you would normally associate with the work of a gun dog.

The Labrador, however, has a lower reactivity to sound, enabling it to cope with gunfire, and its lower body sensitivity makes it better at crashing through thick undergrowth and plunging into cold water. More importantly, the Labrador has a stronger drive to retrieve. You are more likely to be greeted by the resident canine holding a toy or a blanket in its mouth when visiting the home of someone who owns a Labrador than you would when visiting the owner of a Collie. But however good at retrieving it may be, the Labrador, unlike the Collie, is useless at herding sheep.

Although all dogs have inherited the full repertoire of behaviour from their wolf ancestors, certain behaviours are more pronounced in certain breeds, and these behaviours are easier to 'trigger'. To understand more about your own dog, or one you intend to own, it would be a helpful to study the history of its breed, and find out what it was used for.

Nature v Nurture

A question that is frequently asked about behaviour is how much is inherited and how much is caused by the environment in which an animal is raised. This is often referred to as the 'nature or

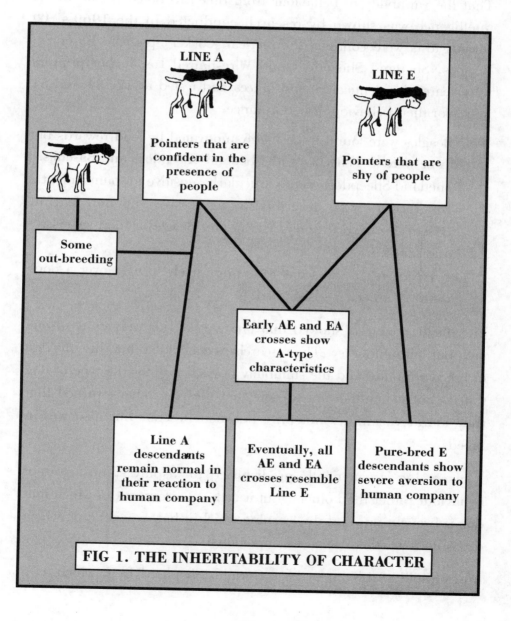

FIG 1. THE INHERITABILITY OF CHARACTER

nurture' argument. That behaviour can be inherited has been shown experimentally in the parallel breeding of two lines of Pointers. (See figure 1 which suggests that the inheritability of nervousness was dominant) [8]

That the variability of behaviour from breed to breed is not due to intelligence was shown by research conducted in the 1960's. [9] Various tests were conducted: American Cocker Spaniels, Basenji's, Beagles, Shetland Sheepdogs and Wire-haired Fox Terrier puppies were reared in identical circumstances and tested at 17, 34 and 51 weeks for their behavioural performance.

- Beagles were found to be highly motivated by food rewards but these were less effective with Shetland Sheepdogs and Basenjis.
- Shetland Sheepdogs were particularly sensitive to 'punishment'.
- Fox Terriers were described as aggressive and non fearful, Basenjis as aggressive and fearful and Beagles as non aggressive and non-fearful.
- Fox Terriers and Basenjis were more likely to fight over a bone than the other breeds studied.

The intelligence tests showed that one type of dog may excel in one area but fail in another. The researchers concluded that this was due to breed variation and the suitability of each task for the type of dog tested. But it is important to note that the researchers warned that they found variability not only between breeds, but also within breeds.

A given dog is genetically predisposed to display some forms of behaviour rather than others. But it is the environment in which that dog is brought up, and the learning which it has experienced, which determines whether it realises its potential.

An example of this might be a German Shepherd Dog, which as a breed has a high potential for territorial behaviour. If the dog lives in the foyer of a busy hotel where strangers come and go all the time, territorial behaviour may not develop because no one seems to be deterred if it barks. If the same dog lives in a yard which strangers frequently pass but rarely enter, territorial behaviour will be more likely to develop because people seem to go away when it barks. If breeds are genetically predisposed to display patterns of behaviour, it follows that the type of problem behaviour displayed by a dog will often be a result of this genetic predisposition. For example, a Border Collie is so keen to herd that it will not only herd sheep but any other livestock whose movement stimulates the response. If it is given inappropriate learning opportunities, the Collie may focus this behaviour onto things whose fast movement causes it to give chase. From a sample 29 cases of inappropriate chase behaviour towards cars, cyclists and joggers that I treated, two thirds of the dogs involved were from the herding breeds.

As dogs are increasingly being kept as pets rather than as workmates, an amenable temperament is becoming a far more important consideration for the owner than the actual breed of the dog. Breeders and fanciers already differentiate between working and non-working lines. How far the behavioural differences between the breeds will become less distinct is likely to be limited by the preferences of the owners and breeders, and of course the genetic correlation between behaviour and the physical aspect of the dog, such as the build of a greyhound and its inherent desire to chase.

It seems then that both genealogy and appropriate learning opportunities are important in the development of a dog's behaviour. This also applies to the development of temperament, and at no time are the appropriate learning opportunities for this more important than in the first few weeks of life.

NOTES

1.   Lorenz K. *Man Meets Dog* (Methuen & Co. London 1954)

2.   Coppinger R., Schneider R. Evolution of Working Dogs in Serpell, J.A. Ed. *The Domestic Dog; Its Evolution, Behaviour and Interactions with People* (Cambridge Univerrsity Press 1995)

3.   Clutton-Brock, J. *Origins of the Dog: Domestication and Early History* in Serpell, J.A. Ed. *The Domestic Dog; Its Evolution, Behaviour and Interactions with People* (Cambridge Univerrsity Press 1995)

4.   Vila C., Savolainen P., Maldonado J.E., Amorim I.R., Rice J.E., Honeycutt R.L.,Crandall K.A., Lundeberg J. and Wayne R.K. Multiple and ancient origins of the domestic dog. **Science** Vol. 276:1687-1689 1997

5.   As note 2.

6.   Robinson I.H. Ed. *The Waltham Book of Human-Animal Interaction* (Pergamon Press Oxford UK)

7.   Messent, P.R. *Correlates and Effects of Pet Ownership in The Pet Connection*, Ed. R.K. Anderson B.L. & L.A. Hart (University of Minnesota 1984)

8.   Murphree O.D. and Dykman R.A. Litter Patterns in the Offspring of Nervous and Stable Dogs 1. Behavioural Tests. **Journal of Nervous and Mental Disease 141,321-322.**

9.   Scott, J.P. & Fuller, J.L. *Genetics and Social behaviour in the Dog* (University of Chicago Press 1965)

———— 2. ————

The Importance of Socialisation and Habituation

In one year I treated 773 dogs. Seventy-nine of them had problems of fearfulness towards people or their environment. This fear appeared to be due to severely restricted experience - interaction with people, with other dogs, with everyday normal life - while they were still puppies. This is just the tip of the iceberg, because many dogs show a weakness of temperament or inability to cope when faced with a particular situation, without their behaviour becoming problematical enough for the owners to seek help.

What are Socialisation and Habituation?

Through **socialisation** an animal learns how to recognise and interact with the species with which it cohabits. In the wild this is likely to be the animal's own species, but for the domestic dog it includes others, such as man and cats. By learning how to interact with other animals, the socialised dog develops communication skills which enable it to recognise the intentions of others and how to respond.

Habituation can be described as the process where an animal becomes accustomed to an environmental stimulus, such as a repeated noise, and learns to ignore it because it is not a threat.

Dogs go through a sensitive period of early development. This is the stage when a dog must learn to adjust to a normal environment, as opposed to the deprivation they often experience in the cages of puppy farms, for example. Socialisation and habituation must occur when the dog is young in order for it not to grow up maladjusted. A maladjusted dog can be improved, but weaknesses are likely to remain.

The degree of deprivation a dog suffers will be reflected proportionately in its fearful response to the things it encounters in later life. These can be anything: men, women, children, heavy goods lorries or a windblown black plastic bag rolling down the street.

- A dog that has had little or no experience will always be inclined to fearfulness without remedial treatment.
- A dog that has had some exposure, but not sufficient, will be better adjusted, although not entirely sound.
- A dog that has had adequate experience will probably grow up to be "bomb-proof", as they say in horsey circles.

Of course this is all dependent upon the individual dog's genetic capacity to develop sound temperament, and the quality of its first experiences.

The evidence which shows the crucial importance of systematically socialising and habituating puppies during the sensitive period has been around for a long time. Dogs develop more gradually than do some other species. Chicks, for example, are able to see and walk when they are born so that they can follow their mother towards food, or out of danger. They must lean quickly to identify their mother: an **imprinting** process by which chicks 'lock on' to their carer - usually the mother - is completed in less than twenty- four hours [1].

The ancestors of puppies, on the other hand, were predators and were therefore at less risk at birth. Consequently a capacity to follow their mother out of danger at such an early age has not evolved. They are born blind, deaf and relatively immobile so are only partially able to start the process of species recognition straight away, by scent.

Research has identified the age of three weeks as the start of a sensitive period [2], during which puppies develop social relationships with the species with which they will live. Significantly, this is also the stage when the puppy becomes truly mobile and can see and hear. Three weeks also coincides with the development of increased electrical activity in the brain [3].

In 1971 a behavioural researcher found that three week old Chihuahua puppies fostered individually in litters of four week old kittens would, by twelve weeks of age, prefer the company of cats to the company of their litter mates that had not been fostered [4]. Additionally, the foster mother's kittens were found to be able to relate to dogs, whereas kittens from other litters who had not had a canine companion thrust upon them avoided contact with dogs.

In the same year, a subtler but even more revealing experiment was carried out. [5] Litters of puppies were split into three groups:

1.   one group of puppies were hand-reared from birth and received no canine contact;

25

2.   the second group were given an equal amount of canine and
      human contact;

3.   the third group only experienced the company of other puppies
      and their dam.

When these three groups of puppies were brought together, those that
had only experienced human interaction preferred the company of
other puppies that had also experienced human company. Similarly,
those puppies exposed to both human and canine company preferred
the company of puppies that had been exposed to the same mixture
of experience, and puppies only used to canine company sought out
similiar playmates.

The most significant tests of all were carried out in the **1960**'s [6].
These found that if puppies were initially kept in isolation from
people, and then subsequently introduced to people at staggered
stages, their responses to these first exposures became progressively
less confident, the older the puppy was.

1.   Those puppies introduced to humans for the first time between
      three to five weeks of age approached confidently.

2.   Those introduced between five and seven weeks of age showed
      increasing amounts of apprehension.

3.   Those puppies whose first experience was at nine weeks or later
      were totally fearful.

It was also found that in puppies kept in isolation from man until
fourteen weeks old, fear and escape responses became so strong that
the puppies continued to behave like wild animals.

So far, the research I have cited has been concerned with aspects of
socialisation. But what of **habituation** - the exposure to environmental stimuli rather than social interaction? Experiments have been
designed to reveal a puppy's sensitive habituation period [7] :

- A group of puppies housed in conditions devoid of stimulation were placed in a test area with various articles for just half an hour at five, eight, twelve and sixteen weeks. It was found that these puppies became progressively keener to explore the items, and that they developed a preference for those items that were more complex.

- Puppies that did not enter the test area until they were over eight weeks old tended to withdraw from rather than explore the items.

- Puppies that did not experience the test area until they were twelve or sixteen weeks old frequently became paralysed with fear.

What does all this research tell us? The main points to bear in mind when considering a dog's behaviour are:

- Even new born puppies can achieve some level of recognition and socialisation to those around them by scent. After all, they have to be able to recognise their mother's warmth and locate the milk bar!

- The sensitive period for socialisation starts at around three weeks, and by eight weeks an inexperienced puppy's response to new stimuli is likely to be fearful.

- The older the puppy is when it starts meeting the world in which it is going to live the less chance there is of it being well adjusted.

Why, one may ask, does a fearful response develop even if puppies don't actually have an unpleasant or fear-evoking experience? One might suppose that puppies would continue to be confident in the presence of all new stimuli if they had not had any unpleasant experiences.

27

One explanation might be that in its natural environment the wolf has to be alert to danger, which means treating anything which is unfamiliar as potentially hazardous. The older the animal is when it encounters a new experience, the more extreme its negative reaction is likely to be. This means that a wolf cub has only a few weeks to develop positive associations with its own kind and immediate environment; it then becomes increasingly cautious about things and situations it has not previously encountered. This saves it from blithely trotting up to something like a snake and investigating it. Those that did not display such caution were less likely to live to pass on the genes our dogs have inherited.

Problems occur because dogs, unlike their ancestors, need to become familiar with an enormous number of stimuli so that they can cope with our rather artificial world. This does not mean that you have to run around and expose your dog to absolutely everything, because to some extent generalisation takes place. For example a puppy's exposure to some noises will help to prepare it for the noisy confusion of traffic.

One interesting experiment [8] (which I don't advise readers to follow) shows how this capacity to cope with life's experiences develops.

- Half of a litter was put in a cold steel bowl for a few minutes each day for a few days.
- The other half of the litter did not have this experience.

When the puppies were tested for their capacity to cope with stress later in life, it was found that the heart rate of those that had received the cold steel bowl experience did not climb as dramatically as those that did not. This suggests that the more a puppy is accustomed to in the first few weeks of life, the more ably it will cope even in unrelated situations. This usefully suggests that a puppy well-used to the sound of the vacuum cleaner, washing machine, television, hi-fi and all the

28

other sounds of family life is better prepared for the world than one kept in a kennel, barn, shed or isolated part of the breeder's home.

Until **1956**, the **Guide Dogs for the Blind Association** used to rely on the donation of adult dogs which they took on approval to maintain their training stock. The success rate of those dogs fluctuated between **9** and **11** percent and it was recognised that this could be improved if the Association could supervise the rearing of puppies. These were purchased and placed in private homes at between ten and twelve weeks old, or even later. Things improved, but the results were not good enough. It was Derek Freeman, who subsequently received an **MBE** for his work, who pushed to have puppies placed in private homes at an earlier age to enable them to receive the maximum socialisation and habituation during the sensitive period of development [9].

Derek found that six weeks was the best time to place puppies in private homes; any later critically reduced the time left before the end of the sensitive period. But if puppies were removed from their dam and litter mates before six weeks, they missed the opportunity to start socialising with their own kind, which resulted in inept interactions with other dogs later in life.

The training success rate soared because of this policy, which was carried out in conjunction with the management of the gene pool via the breeding scheme Derek also pioneered. Annual success rates in excess of **75** percent became common. Today most guide dogs are born into the domestic environment of the brood bitch holder's home rather than the kennel environment that was the norm when the breeding and rearing scheme was first started.

You might think that because this is a special scheme for dogs with a special function it is not necessary to manage dogs that are to become household pets in the same way. In fact, what the scheme provides is simply adult dogs that are of sound temperament. It is these dogs coincidentally that make the best material for training as guide dogs.

As a result of the breeding scheme, Derek Freeman also proved, if proof was needed, that you cannot dismiss the importance of genetic predisposition. That is to say, the basic material required for good temperament can be produced through good breeding. Conversely, a lack of habituation and socialisation can ruin the chance of a dog developing a sound temperament, however good the genealogy.

Before I turn to other questions, there is one more line of research that must be mentioned because it introduces another parameter within which dog owners, breeders and trainers are obliged to work if a puppy's potential is to be maximised. The research has revealed the fact that socialisation and habituation of puppies can wear off.[10] The researchers found that wolf cubs that had been socialised up to twelve to fourteen weeks, lost their socialising capacity when interaction with the researchers was withdrawn.

It has subsequently been found [11] that that if well-socialised puppies are placed in a kennel environment between three and four months of age, and left there in virtual isolation until they are between six and eight months of age, they will be shy of strangers and even of their caretakers, if they have not been handled by them very much during that time. Well-socialised puppies of six months old or more left in the same surroundings for two months do not lose their confidence. More recent research suggests that socialisation and habituation has to be continually reinforced throughout the juvenile period until maturity.

Let us consider just two examples of how this affects us as dog owners.

1.   A puppy, well socialised until it is twelve weeks old, will require

the socialisation to continue until it is mature, for the full benefits to be achieved.

2. The same rule applies to a puppy that has been habituated to hearing traffic in the first few weeks of life. If it is then kept in a quiet rural environment until it is six or more months old it is likely to become fearful in the presence of traffic unless its owners ensure that it has periodic exposure to traffic by taking it to where traffic will be encountered.

The most worrying result of a failure to socialise and habituate is that a dog fearful of a person or an object will naturally want to move away from it to maintain a safe distance. If flight is denied the dog has three options; to accept the person or item, to continue to struggle to get away, or to try and make the person or item go away.

In the last case the dog will often use aggression. Significantly, most of the dogs referred to me who are fearful because of a lack of sociali- sation and habituation display aggression towards the things they are frightened of. Fear aggression is discussed in detail in ch. 15.

Everything I have stated so far leads to this question: why, if the benefits of socialisation and habituation are so irrefutably proven, are so many dogs under-socialised and habituated in the first few weeks of life? The reasons vary, but an examination of the early history of the seventy-nine dogs I mentioned at the beginning of this chapter shows that they fall into two main categories. I will refer to them as groups A and B:

A: Dogs that are retained by the breeder in an environment **devoid** of stimulation or with **limited** stimulation until well into, or past, the sensitive period.

B: Those that have been retained in the new owner's household until the puppy's vaccination programme is complete, often long after the sensitive period has passed.

	No. of Dogs	Age acquired by owners	Puppy's Environment
group A	4	Up to 10 weeks	Barn or shed
	6	10-12 weeks	Kennel or outhouse equivalent
	16	12-16 weeks	Kennel or breeder's home
	15	Over 16 weeks	Kennel or breeder's home
group B	38	6-12 weeks	Retained within new owner's home until vaccinations complete often, after 16 weeks of age

Of those dogs in group A we have to take into account the fact that breeders sometimes cannot find enough suitable homes quickly enough. Having said that, it is unfortunate that some of them believe that most families are unsuitable to look after a puppy when it is six weeks old, although it is difficult to see what suddenly makes them suitable when the puppy is eight, ten or twelve weeks old.

All too often, breeders, unaware of the harm they are doing, retain puppies well into and sometimes past the sensitive socialisation and habituation period so that they have time to choose which puppy or puppies they wish to keep for showing before launching the rest on

32

the unsuspecting public. However there is nothing wrong in a breeder retaining a puppy for as long as he or she wants, as long as it is ensured that each puppy is properly socialised and habituated as an individual. Each puppy needs to learn to cope with the environment without the support of its litter brothers and sisters. Although this is possible, it is, in practice, very time consuming.

In group B, the implementation of vaccination programmes was a major contributor to the number of psychologically disturbed puppies. This was done in the name of the puppy's physiological well-being, which is essential, but we don't have to choose between physical well-being and the benefits of socialisation and habituation. To understand why there has been a problem in the past we need to know something of the principles and the history of puppy vaccination.

When a bitch has a litter she passes immunity (antibodies) to infectious diseases such as distemper and parvovirus via her placenta (10%) and more importantly via her milk (90%) to her puppies. The immunity puppies obtain from her gradually declines, and to stop them becoming vulnerable to infectious diseases, immunity is re established by vaccination. However, whilst a puppy still has an effective amount of the immunity acquired from its mother the antibodies cancel out any vaccination given, making it difficult for vets to know when to vaccinate.

In the 1950's a scientist named Baker showed that by twelve weeks of age 98% of puppies have lost their maternally derived immunity to infection, which means that if puppies are vaccinated at twelve weeks, the vaccine would have a high take-up rate. To ensure that the puppies were not exposed to sources of infection in the meantime they were isolated in the owner's household until they were at least twelve weeks old, and normally for two or more weeks after that.

This practice still lingers on. While it is undoubtedly cost effective, it completely ignores the puppy's psychological needs. Once again, it was Derek Freeman who pioneered the way forward [12]. He had an urgent need to start socialising and habituating puppies within the sensitive period, i.e. from six weeks onwards, but of course he still had to ensure their protection from infection.

After consultation with one of the drug companies that produced puppy vaccines, blood samples were taken from bitches that were in whelp so that their antibody level could be counted. The lower the count in a bitch's blood sample, the smaller the amount of immunity the puppies would gain from her milk. Consequently the actual time the puppies' vaccination programme should start could be predicted, and generally speaking it proved to be around six weeks. Subsequent research has confirmed that most puppies have lost an effective level of maternally derived antibodies by six weeks of age.

The Guide Dogs for the Blind Association developed a policy of systematically vaccinating all puppies at six weeks, and then repeating the process at intervals to catch those few whose level of maternally derived immunity was too high for a vaccine to take on the first occasion. This removed the need to blood test every bitch for a count of antibodies. The policy ensured that at any one time puppies were covered, either by maternal antibodies or the vaccine.

In more recent years vaccines have been specifically designed for early use. They are able to overcome what is known as the immunity gap. This is the period of time in which the puppy's maternally derived antibodies are too low in number to prevent infection, but numerous enough to kill off any vaccine given. Whatever system of early vaccination is used, multiple or specific early cover, the principle has been proved as a safe and effective means of ensuring that puppies receive early socialisation and habituation in the world beyond their owners home. Derek Freeman stated that apart from when parvovirus first appeared, for which there was no protection at the time, he could count on the fingers of one hand the number of puppies that became unwell out of the thousands that had gone though the breeding scheme.

It must be remembered that vaccination programmes have to be carried out under strict veterinary supervision and have to be boosted annually. The vet's opinion is also important because some areas of some towns put a puppy at higher risk of infection than others. A puppy's safety can be further assured by carrying it in a blanket until its vaccination programme is complete. The blanket will not only keep the puppy warm, but it will also absorb the puppy's toileting, thereby eliminating the need of the owner to put the puppy on the ground where it could be exposed to sources of infection, such as locations where other dogs have defecated or urinated.

NOTES

1.	Lorens, K.; cited in Drickamer L.C., Vessey S.H. and Meikle D. *Animal Behaviour* 4th Ed. (W. C. Brown, USA, 1996)

2.	Freedman, D.G. King J.A. Elliot, O. 'Critical Period in the Social Development of Dogs', **Science** Vol. 133, pp. 1016-1017.(1961)

	Scott, J.P. Fuller J.L. *Genetics and Social Development of the Dog* (University of Chicago Press, 1965)

3.	Fox, M.W. *The Dog: Its Domestication and Behaviour* (Garland S & P.M. Press, N.Y., 1978)

4.	As 3.

5.	As 3.

6.	As 2.

7.	As 3.

8.	Fox, M.W. *Understanding Your Dog* (Coward, McCann and Geoghegan Inc., N.Y., 1972)

9.   Freeman, D. *Barking Up the Right Tree* (Ringpress, Letchworth, Herts., 1991)

10. Woolpy, J.H. 'Socialisation of Wolves' in *Animal and Human*, ed. J.H. Masserman (Grune & Stratton 1968)

11. Fox, M. (1971); cited in Sautter F.J. & Glover J.A., *Behaviour, Development and Training of the Dog* (Arco Publishing, N.Y. 1978)

12. As 9

——3.——

How To Introduce A Puppy To The World

Now we have looked at the theoretical aspects of early socialisation and habituation, let us see how we can put them to practical use.

To ensure the best chance of developing sound temperament and capacity to cope in all circumstances, a puppy's exposure to the environment in which it is going to live should be as systematic as possible.

Early Days

A lot of the responsibility for ensuring that a puppy gets a good start lies with the breeder; and this responsibility begins before the birth of the pup, with the selection of a dam and sire whose genetic make-up will be best suited to produce puppies of good temperament; but the process continues the moment a puppy is born, when it starts to get used to the breeder's scent and to being handled.

The routines that are normally used to assist in whelping are enough to accomplish this - any more unnecessary interference may distress the mother.

As the puppy and its litter mates grow up, the breeder should increase the amount of handling the puppies receive, and to introduce interaction with other people. If the breeder is a woman, for example, and she is the only, or main, human contact the puppies have, they are likely to be less well-adjusted towards men and children. It is sensible in these circumstances to invite men and children into the household to see and handle the puppies on a regular basis, particularly if the puppies remain with the breeder after they are six weeks old. It is, of course, important that the vet's advice on hygiene procedures is sought to prevent the introduction of infectious disease.

Taking trouble to ensure early and comprehensive socialisation is in the breeder's own interests. Many woman breeders, for example, complain that their dog "will not show under a male judge". Often this is because the dog is fearful of men to some extent, due to a lack of socialisation with them. This can result in apprehensive behaviour at the best of times, but when a male judge is in the show ring staring at the dog and attempting to touch it, there need be little wonder that it cannot cope.

I have seen some extreme examples of dogs that are afraid of men. One case involved a Great Dane that was reared by a breeder who lived on her own. It was subsequently sold to an elderly lady who lived on her own in a rural environment. By about twenty weeks of age the puppy's owner decided that she would not be able to cope with such a large dog when it grew up and it was re-homed with a young family in a city suburb. I saw the dog two weeks later. He was able to cope with the mother of the family, and he was not too nervous with the children who were about five and seven years old; but he was absolutely petrified of the father. As soon as the father walked into the room, the dog would hide under or behind the nearest piece of furniture. The dog was treated successfully, but it took a long time and it could all have been avoided through a little forward planning at the puppy stage.

It is also important for breeders to ensure that the puppies in their care get enough stimulation from their environment. Not being able to take them away from the premises in the first six weeks is limiting, but a puppy that has had regular experience of a busy domestic environment will be more able to cope with the world than one that has been shut away in a quiet kennel or isolated room. Audio tapes of environmental stimuli such as traffic noises, vacuum cleaners, washing machines, etc, can be made and played to puppies kept in isolated locations, but the associated visual and olfactory experiences are important too. Tapes can also be useful if a puppy is unwell of for some other reason cannot be taken outside the home.

Good breeders will make themselves responsible for acquainting new owners with the principles of socialisation and habituation at the same time that they advise on diet and other details. It is also a good idea for them to ensure that prospective owners have enough time and dedication to continue the socialisation and habituation process properly, because if they don't, and if the puppy subsequently develops a less than sound temperament, it may be that the dog's breeding, unjustifiably, gets the blame.

Prospective owners can maximise their opportunities to socialise and habituate their puppies by obtaining them at six weeks old, having already made arrangements for the appropriate vaccination programme with a vet. Of course, failing to obtain a puppy at exactly six weeks of age does not lead to disaster; but the greater the age of the puppy, the more precious time you will have lost. With luck this will have been countered to some extent by the level of sensory stimulation the breeder has provided; but if a puppy has been raised in an environment devoid of stimulation, such as in a barn or a quiet kennel, then starting wider socialisation and habituation at six weeks is critically important.

If you are a prospective purchaser, you can check that some degree of socialisation and habituation has already taken place. Seek out a breeder who will let you see the puppies with their dam in their living quarters prior to the optimum homing age of six weeks. You can ask the breeder how much human handling, canine interaction and general exposure to the world the puppies have had, but the proof of the pudding is the reaction of the puppies themselves.

- They should appear to be content and confident.
- A few simple tests, such as the clapping of hands and the dropping of car keys will enable you to gauge how well habituated the puppies are. Observe whether they move away from the sound or towards it to investigate it. A mild interest in the sound and a quick recovery from the surprise is ideal.
- They should also be willing to approach and investigate you and be happy to allow themselves to be handled. Be wary of a shy puppy.
- Observe the behaviour of the dam and any other dogs that live in the vicinity of the puppies. If the puppies have grown up in the company of a nervous or aggressive dog they may have learnt fear or aggression from its example and it may be wiser to look elsewhere for a puppy than to take the risk.

Many guides have been written on how to choose an individual puppy from the litter, and they tend to recommend that an inexperienced owner avoid the most forward puppy, because it is likely to grow up as dominant, and may prove difficult to handle. However, research has shown [1] that the hierarchical structure of a seven week old litter varies from day to day, because the puppies are still developing the way they interact with each member of the group. This was still found to be the case at ten weeks of age. So when choosing a puppy, bear the above points in mind, and consider whether the puppy is a suitable choice to fit in with your home and life-style: how large will it grow, how much exercise will it require, etc. Be ruled by your head and not your heart. Your heart can take over once the choice has been made.

If you are about to purchase a puppy, or if, as a breeder, you intend to keep a puppy until it is older to see how it develops, there is a lot you will have to consider, such as toilet training, preventing chewing and how to get a good night's sleep. In the upheaval, time must be put aside to consider the best locations for socialising and habituating your puppy. The guidelines below should help you.

If you own another dog or dogs, remember that your puppy will need opportunities to meet experiences on its own so that it learns to cope as an individual rather than depend on its companion when it is stressed.

Things you can do at home

Visitors

- Accustom your puppy to lots of visitors of both sexes and all ages. This will develop its social experience and help to keep territorial behaviour to manageable levels in later life.

Children

- Accustom your puppy to being handled by your children and/or other people's children, but remain in a position of supervision and don't let them pester it or treat it as a toy.

- Arrange to meet someone with a baby regularly so that your puppy can get used to these sights and sounds. This can be especially important if you plan to have a family, because it will help to overcome the common worries about how the family dog will react to a new baby and toddlers. The subject of dogs and babies is discussed more fully at the end of this chapter.

Grooming

- Groom your puppy every day, even if it is of a smooth-haired or wire-haired breed which may not seem to need it. Grooming will accustom your puppy to being thoroughly handled; and, incidentally, it will help prevent the development of dominant behaviour.

Veterinary examination

- Every day examine your puppy's ears, eyes, teeth, lift up its feet and check its paws, and check under its tail. When your puppy is happy about this, get other people to do it (it makes a good talking point at dinner parties: "Pass the croutons, please, ...and, by the way, have you looked under Bonzo's tail lately?") The purpose of the exercise is to accustom your puppy to veterinary examination. This is very important, especially if First Aid has to be administered in a hurry.

Domestic sights and sounds

- Expose your puppy to domestic stimuli such as the vacuum cleaner, spin drier etc; but don't make an issue of them. The puppy should get used to them gradually without being stressed.

The postman, milkman etc.

- Take your puppy outside and meet these people as often as you can. If your puppy gets to know and like them it will be less likely to show territorial aggression towards them when it grows up. (Some householders have to collect their post from the sorting office because the postman will no longer deliver to their home as a result of their dog's behaviour). This will work better if you can encourage them to feed your puppy titbits - if not, feed the pup yourself while meeting them, so that a pleasant association develops.

Cats

- If you have a cat, introduce your puppy to it. Keep the puppy under control and reward it for not pestering. Be careful not to worry the cat, as it may scratch your puppy. Placing the cat in a cat carrying basket just out of the puppy's reach, or putting the puppy in an indoor kennel can be useful methods of introduction with little chance of an unpleasant incident occurring. This can be repeated at intervals for a few days so that both puppy and cat learn to become settled in each other's company.

Other dogs at home

- If you already have a dog, introduce your puppy to it in the garden. Keep the older dog on a lead if you think extra care is necessary. Once the initial acceptance has been made by the older dog, the two should work out their relationship and settle down without too much intervention from you.

Preventing play-biting

- See page.54

Leash training

- Prepare your puppy for walking on the lead by getting it used to its collar and lead in the garden.

Going solo

- Socialisation is very important, but so is learning to remain relaxed when left alone. A puppy which is not accustomed to being left unattended on a regular basis is much more likely to suffer from separation anxiety (i.e. become anxious when separated from the owner because it is over-attached) in adulthood.

To help prevent your puppy from suffering from this very common syndrome, you need to leave it unattended (i.e. in the house on its own), preferably in the area where it sleeps overnight. This should not be your bedroom, as sleeping there can contribute to separation anxiety and other problems. To help a very young puppy taken from its dam settle at night in its new basket or kennel, wrap an alarm clock and a hot water bottle together in an old woolly jumper, and let the puppy sleep against this warm, ticking parcel. It will comfort the puppy by simulating its mother's heartbeat. Remember not to set the alarm, however! The parcel can be removed when the puppy is a little older, and more independent and confident. You can also use other, safe heat sources, such as placing the puppy's bed next to a warm radiator overnight.

For your puppy's safety, to prevent it from relieving itself in inappropriate places, and to keep it from chewing inappropriate items, ensure its area is "chew-proof" and free from hazards such as electrical cables.

- You may need to construct or buy some purpose-built barriers to make a pen.

- You could use a child gate to keep it in a small, chew-proof room; some owners, for instance, use their utility room.
- Indoor kennels are often used, and are the best option.

Leave your puppy with some appropriate chew items, such as long-lasting chews from the pet shop, and some fresh water.

You should start to accustom your puppy to separation from you during the day by sitting in the same room whilst it is in its pen or indoor kennel, or in the next room if you are using a child gate.

Over a period of time you can build up the routine to the point where you can sit in another room with the door between you shut. Once your puppy accepts this you can start to leave the house; go next door for a coffee, for example. Gradually extend the time you are away until you are absent for over an hour on a regular basis.

- The best time to carry out this training is when your puppy looks sleepy.
- Do not go back if you hear your puppy crying. Return when it is quiet. If a puppy finds it can call you back or get you to talk to it, even if it is only to tell it to be quiet, it may never accept being left without making a noise.
- Keep your rate of progress at a level that is consistent with the development of your puppy's capacity to cope without you, so that it remains relaxed. (Also see Separation Problems in Chapter 16)
- When your puppy is very young, you can leave it with a cloth to lie on, freshly impregnated with your scent. Research has shown [2] that there is often a link to a dog's over-attachment to a particular member of the household and separation anxiety. (Whether this is a symptom of impending separation

problems, or a consequence of them, is not clear.) Wherever possible, help to prevent this by sharing responsibility for caring, feeding and walking the dog with other members of the household.

Further research has shown a link between an illness during the first few weeks of life and some cases of separation problems later on. [3] Although it is not yet clear what this research implies in terms of interacting with a sick puppy, it is probably a good idea not to mother the puppy over-much, and to avoid inducing stress by enforced separation during the puppy's illness.

Things to do away from home

Go to all the places you can think of that will help your puppy become 'bomb proof'. Start in quieter places and gradually progress to busier ones. Expose your puppy to the sound of traffic and the movement of people. Start in quiet side streets and gradually build up to busy ones. Places where people congregate are also valuable experience. Any environment where people tend to congregate to sit and chat will do, so that they have the time to take interest in and handle your puppy.

Children

Let children approach and pet your puppy. Control their enthusiasm to prevent the puppy from being overwhelmed. Make sure your puppy has been wormed before bringing it into contact with children of any age.

The car

- Plenty of car travel will accustom your puppy to it.
- Do not let your puppy sit on the front seat or on someone's lap.

Get it accustomed to travelling in the place which it will occupy when it is an adult.

The countryside

* Get your puppy accustomed to the sights, sounds and smells of the countryside, livestock etc. But be careful to keep it under control, on a lead.
* Reward it for ignoring livestock. A puppy or dog not on a lead or under close control in the vicinity of livestock can be shot on sight by the farmer, so in your enthusiasm don't forget the Country Code.

Leash training

Once your vet has said that your puppy can be safely walked on a lead instead of being carried, then you should repeat the earlier routine. Go back to using quiet areas, then gradually build up to noisy and busy ones again. In addition, think about the unusual places to which you can introduce your puppy. Open staircases, for example, can be challenging. Accustom your puppy to a range of unusual experiences, such as the vibration of station platforms when trains arrive, or the movement of the floors on trains, buses and lifts. All these and similar experiences will help to develop its confidence.

Kennels

See the section about kennels on page.62

Socialising with other dogs

As we have seen, removing a puppy from its dam and litter mates at six weeks is ideal in terms of socialising it with people and broadening its experience of the environment, but its socialisation with other dogs stops and begins to wear off. This means that some steps have to be taken to ensure that the process of learning to interact with others dogs continues, if you don't want your dog to become maladjusted.

However, socialising with other dogs does not mean letting your puppy run amok with other dogs in the park. If the other dogs are not properly socialised, their communication skills may be poor, which can often result in misunderstanding and aggression, and this sort of encounter can result in a puppy learning to be aggressive towards other dogs that it meets.

In order that your puppy's canine interaction skills can be properly developed, it is very important to locate and attend one of the increasingly popular puppy socialisation classes (see Chapter 9), even if it means travelling some distance to get there. At the end of this book there is a list of useful addresses, including that of the Association of Pet Behaviour Counsellors, which can provide advice on finding a puppy class near you.

What should you do if a puppy shows fear whilst it is being socialised/habituated?

A   Do not overreact. If you try to reassure a puppy it may reinforce its fear. It may also interpret your reassurance as your own fearful response to the thing that frightened it. As "pack leader" you should appear to be unaffected and unworried so as to set an example.

B   Do not try to force a puppy into approaching whatever is frightening it, as you will highlight its fear.

C   Expose your puppy to the type of stimulus that worries it as often as possible, but initially from a distance (thus reducing the level of stimulation) so that the puppy can become desensitised to it. As your puppy's reaction improves you can gradually increase the amount of exposure it has.

D   Reward the puppy every time it does not react to the stimulus, or as soon as it recovers from its fright if it does react.

Preventing chewing, house soiling and play biting

Chewing

When you get a new puppy, you have a chance to go through the fun and frustrations of teaching it how to behave the way you want when it is indoors. Although this is of course worthwhile, it takes up precious time; and, even then, it is unlikely that you can be on hand at all hours. You can save a lot of time and heartache by introducing a simple - though unfortunately expensive - item of equipment to your household: an indoor kennel. As an added bonus, an indoor kennel will give you peace of mind through knowing that your puppy is safe and not chewing through your wiring.

Indoor kennels are collapsible cages made of metal. They come in various sizes, but when folded away even the biggest does not take up much room. If you do not want to go to the expense of an indoor kennel you can create the equivalent by adapting a chew-proof area in your home. However, an indoor kennel has an advantage in that it can be moved from one place to another, which is useful if you are visiting somebody's home. They can also be sold on when they are no longer needed, or stored away until the next time you decide to have a puppy.

The indoor kennel is a useful place for your puppy to sleep in, and it can be popped in whenever it can't be supervised for short periods of time, and overnight. As a result it will not chew the things you do not want it to when you are not looking; nor will it associate the wrong materials (such as your shoes or the furniture) with chewing, and so get into bad habits. This may not seem to be very important in the first few weeks because your puppy is so small and can do little damage; but it may become important as it gets bigger and has a desperate need to chew things when it starts teething.

Your puppy will need to have some things it can chew, so place items such as rawhide chews, sterilised bones and those products designed for dogs to chew on, inside the kennel. This will not only help it with those vital chewing exercises; it will also help it learn to associate chewing with those items.

When you find yourself chasing after your puppy to reclaim the things it has pinched or to stop it chewing the wrong things when it is out of the kennel, you can orientate it back to the right things by bringing them out of the kennel and encouraging your puppy to show an interest in them. Wherever possible, make sure the right things to chew are available wherever your puppy is, and give it praise and attention when it is chewing them.

House training

House training can so easily be stress-free and mess-free - if you know how!

Puppy puddles and other little accidents are things that are to be expected during the house training process but eventually most puppies become house trained, often despite what their owners do rather than because of it. Getting the training right will speed up the process and make it less likely that either you or your puppy will get stressed in the meantime.

In particular, bear in mind that the idea that a puppy should be punished when it has an 'accident' is an old wives' tale. Barbaric practices such as rubbing its nose in the offending mess, or showing it the puddle and shouting, may relieve some owner's frustration; but the puppy will just get anxious, and it will not learn anything. Its anxiety may even retard its capacity to control its bladder.

It is important to remember that a dog can only associate an action with its consequences if they occur within half a second of each other. If your dog's ears are down and it is slinking, it is displaying submissive behaviour, not guilt. (See Chapter 4).

Dogs are naturally inhibited about fouling the area where they live and sleep. A few dogs have problems because of the environment where they spent the first few months of life - such as living in an upstairs flat where it is difficult for the dog to learn to 'ask' to go out because the door to the outside world is so far away from the area in which it lives. In particular, a puppy that has lived in a kennel environment for too long can have problems because there is no chance for it to develop the inhibition about fouling the core area of the living space.

New-born puppies' defecation and urination are stimulated by the licking actions of their dam, who cleans up after them. As the puppies become more mobile they start to move away from the nest to relieve themselves. The older and bigger they become, the further away they want to go. Unless you happen to have a west wing it can use, it is more likely than not that your dog will eventually want to relieve itself outside.

At night an indoor kennel will restrict the space available, so your puppy will be inhibited about toileting in it. In consequence, the pup will quickly learn to wait to go outside. At first you will have to make a point of getting up early to let your puppy out, but as it becomes increasingly able to restrain itself, you can gradually adjust the timing until it matches the time when you usually get up.

If you have a dog flap, house-training during the day can be practically painless because it is easy to make a pen just inside the door. The puppy can be put inside the pen whenever it cannot be supervised. Given the choice between its bed or the garden, the puppy will train itself to go outside.

As discussed in chapter 5 puppies can be trained to relieve themselves on newspaper, placed near their sleeping area. As soon as the association between toileting and paper has been made, the paper is gradually moved nearer the door, and then placed outside. Although this is a positive training technique, it sometimes fails because the puppy learns that it is acceptable to make a mess in the house and never progresses to the next stage of 'asking' to be let outside.

One of the best ways of developing good house training is to prevent bad habits forming by not letting your puppy foul in the wrong place whenever possible.

As soon as your puppy has woken up, has finished eating, or is let out of its pen or indoor kennel, it is almost certain to want to relieve itself. You should straightaway take it to the area you want it to use, such as your garden. This will help it learn to associate that place with toileting behaviour.

At other times you should be able to tell when your puppy needs to relieve itself by watching closely. You may see increased restlessness, sniffing, circling and finally movement towards a squatting or crouching position. Interrupt immediately either by lifting your puppy up, or, if it is old enough, by encouraging it to the door that gives access to the garden or other area you want it to use.

If your puppy or older dog does have an 'accident' inside, it is sensible to reduce the possibility of a repeat performance by removing the smell. Suitable methods are:

- An enzymic cleaner, such as a proprietary product you can obtain from your vet
- A 10% solution of biological washing powder.

Either of these will help to break down any deposits and prevent any residual smell. Detergents and bleaches are not so suitable because your puppy may associate the smell they leave behind with defecating; and so it will be attracted back to the same spot to relieve itself.

Although the act of relieving itself should be rewarding enough to encourage your puppy to use the correct area, you can add an extra incentive by praising it, producing a toy from your pocket and initiating a game, or by giving a titbit as your puppy finishes relieving itself in the correct place. In time your puppy will learn that the quicker it relieves itself, the sooner the good things will happen. If it does not 'perform' within three minutes or so, it should be taken back indoors until it next shows signs of wanting to relieve itself. This will prevent it from learning that the longer it dithers and fails to perform, the longer it can keep you standing in the garden and receive your undivided attention.

The same principle applies to those people who have to take their dog for a walk for it to relieve itself (armed, naturally, with poop scoop or plastic bag). On these occasions it is important not to fall into the trap of walking home immediately your dog has performed because some dogs learn to associate toileting with the end of the walk and 'hang on' for as long as they can, because then the walk lasts longer. This might result in the dog toileting when it gets home! It is much better to go to a suitable area and start the walk properly once your dog has relieved itself. This will teach it that the sooner it performs the quicker it can get on with the walk.

Toileting on Demand

It is a good idea to teach your puppy or dog to relieve itself when you give it a signal, which you can do in much the same way as you can teach it to sit or lie down. Guide dogs, for example, are taught the signal 'get busy'. You can do this by repeating a 'buzz' word just as it starts to relieve itself. Eventually your dog will associate the sound of the word with the action and you can use the word to trigger it. This can be particularly useful when you are away from home and you need your dog to relieve itself in a location it has not previously associated with toileting.

Play Biting And Mouthing

In a pack, as soon as puppies become active they play physical games with each other, and they can pester the adults by pulling their ears, tails etc. In their early days puppies have license to do what they like but, as they grow up, adults and litter mates alike become increasingly intolerant of their sharp teeth. So puppies learn that other individuals react to their biting behaviour, and they learn to control the strength they use. By eighteen weeks they have learned that hard mouthing or play-biting is taboo, and that a rebuff will quickly follow any transgression of the rules.

When a puppy is introduced into the family this learning process is normally incomplete and the family must take over where the puppy's mother and litter mates left off. How is this done?

The simple way is for the person concerned to respond with a sharp "No!" as if they have been hurt whenever the puppy uses its teeth in play or mouths them. They should then walk off and ignore the puppy for a few moments. In this way the puppy should learn to limit the strength of its bite in play and that, if it bites someone in earnest who upsets it, it does not have to bite hard to get an effect.

Sometimes, however, a more sophisticated approach is required because the puppy continues to bite despite our best efforts.It may have turned the procedure above into a game, or have learned to do it as an attention seeking device. You can prevent or rectify this by teaching the dog the word 'off'. To do this:

• Hold a titbit between finger and thumb just in front of your dog's or puppy's face	• Each time it tries to snatch it pull your hand upwards and out of reach whilst quietly saying the word 'off'.

After many repetitions it will learn to respond to the sound of the word 'off' by turning its face away from your hand or by stepping back.

The titbit should only be given using the words 'take it' when your dog or puppy makes no attempt to snatch at it. After several of these training sessions the word 'off' can then be used to get your dog to pull its mouth back, or respond to the word 'off' in other situations such as when it is play-biting or jumping up on you or on a work surface. A further benefit of this exercise is that it can help your puppy or dog learn how to cope with frustration.

Dogs and Children

The expression "child substitute" is often used with reference to dogs belonging to childless owners. Sometimes the description is accurate because a dog can become a focus for the owners' maternal and paternal drives to nurture. In today's Western society families are so scattered geographically that the opportunity to have a hand in the raising of the children of close relatives, an act that would have helped to fulfil this need, is a rarity. Added to this phenomenon is the fact that modern social trends have produced an army of potential parents who postpone procreation in favour of furthering their careers, or who wish to avoid the demands made on their resources and social lives. One must also acknowledge the fact that in some cases couples are sadly unable to have children. Whatever the reason that children are absent from a household, the situation can leave a void in the fulfilment of adult needs, and the problem is sometimes partly resolved by obtaining a dog.

Everything goes smoothly for a while and the happy owners admit that they treat Fido like a baby, lavishing on him all that is due to their first born. The problems often start when all of a sudden everything *is* due to the first born. At this point concern starts about

how Fido will take to the arrival of a baby. This anxiety tends to be particularly acute if Fido has not been too happy about babies he has met in the past. Concerns can also be aroused if it is thought that Fido will be jealous of the baby. These concerns are also triggered in dog owners who are prospective grandparents, contemplating how family visits will go once the baby is born. In most cases these and other concerns prove to be totally unfounded, however a few simple precautions will reduce the risk of problems occurring.

As discussed in the chapter on socialisation, exposing a puppy to the presence of babies and supervised socialisation with young children during its first few weeks of life and thereafter, will help to prevent the development of fear. This may not be easy to arrange, but you should try because a dog is less likely to react apprehensively to the presence of babies and toddlers if it is familiar with the experience.

Once you know a baby is on the way you can do a variety of things to prepare your dog for its arrival. For example, if your dog is used to receiving your attention on demand, and physical contact whenever you sit down, some adjustment may have to be made because the baby will reduce your availability. Logically it must be kinder to the dog to make this a gradual adjustment before the baby arrives, rather than a sudden one after the event. To help your dog adjust you can develop a policy of giving it attention only when you initiate it, rather than when your dog seeks it. This does not imply that your dog will receive no attention; you can fuss it as much as you want when you initiate the activity.

You can take the preparation process further by acting out some of the routines that will preoccupy you when the baby arrives to familiarise your dog with them. Examples include pretending to feed by cradling a blanket in the appropriate position, and if you can cope with the bizarre nature of the idea, talking to it. Other routines that can be practised include coo-cooing in the baby's cot, kneeling on the floor and folding up clothes to simulate changing routines etc. Although your dog will not be fooled into thinking there is a baby there it will have the chance to become accustomed to a change in your behaviour and preoccupation.

You can also accustom your dog to some of the environmental experiences that are to invade the home. Perhaps the most significant of these is the sound of a baby crying which can agitate some dogs. Desensitisation can be achieved in part by using a tape recording of a baby crying; your midwife may be able to help you get a recording. Initially the tape should be played very quietly, and you should give your dog attention every so often when you are sure it is ignoring the sound to encourage it to ignore the sound on future occasions. Over the course of a few days the volume can be gradually increased. If possible the smell of a baby can also be introduced into the house on clothes borrowed from other parents. Although this will not be the smell of your own baby, there will be some things in common such as the smell of nappies, wipes and lotions etc.

How to First Introduce the Dog and Baby

The best approach is to act as if there is nothing of any significance the dog would want to react to. This means that when the baby and dog are first brought together those people present should behave in a nonchalant fashion, neither encouraging the dog to take an interest nor shunning it. If you are unsure how your dog will respond you can initially keep it on a lead until it is apparent that everything is allright. However if your dog shows excessive interest in the baby or the sound of crying, taped or real, despite attempts to adopt the best approach, some professional guidance may be necessary to help settle things down (See Further Help on page.281).

Once in-laws and family friends know that the new baby is home they will naturally want to see it. If your dog has always received a lot of attention on the arrival of these visitors it might find it difficult to adjust to their altered priorities. To prevent this causing a problem it is advantageous to ensure that these visitors greet the dog as they normally would, before getting the elated greeting and baby talk out of their systems. A suitable alternative to this arrangement might be for a member of your family to take the dog for a walk just before the visitors are due to arrive, and time the walk so that all the fuss will have settled down by the time it gets home.

New mothers sometimes find that coping with a demanding or problematical dog and a baby can be difficult. If your dog is unable to jump a child gate the occasional use of one can be an invaluable method of providing potentially fractious parents with a time-out facility. Although a closed door will do just as well, the use of a child gate may be a less stressful means of segregation for your dog because it can retain some contact with you. Ideally your dog should be accustomised to this arrangement for short periods of time before the baby arrives. Once the baby has arrived it should only be necessary to prevent your dog's access to you for short periods of time. This facility - or the more expensive option of an indoor kennel - will allow you to concentrate on your parental tasks without having to worry what your dog is doing all the time, e.g. stealing the baby's toys to get your attention, or scavenging the baby's food. It also makes it easier to ensure that you never have to leave your dog and baby unattended in the same room. Once the baby starts to crawl the tables are turned, and the gate can provide the dog with an area into which it can be allowed to escape from clutching little fingers.

The next watershed your family will cross will be when your baby starts to crawl and toddle. Whereas your dog may be able to cope with a relatively immobile baby, this uncoordinated thing coming towards it could be an entirely different matter. What is more there is no escape.

Jemima runs screaming into the lounge where her mother, Mrs Green, is drinking coffee and chatting with her next door neighbour, Mrs Sweet, whose house they are in. There is blood running down Jemima's cheek and a small cut just above her eye. Tearfully, she blurts out that Jack, Mrs Sweet's Jack Russell, has just bitten her.

Horrified, Mrs Sweet is full of remorse and apologetic for Jack's behaviour. Mrs Green is too concerned for Jemima to take much notice of the apology and rushes her four year old daughter to the hospital, where Jemima is given two butterfly stitches.

That night, Mr and Mrs Sweet are confronted by an irate Mr

Green standing on their doorstep demanding that Jack is put to sleep to prevent the incident from being repeated.

Heartbroken, the next day Mr and Mrs Sweet reluctantly comply with his wishes to avoid the legal action the Greens are threatening.

Poor Jack. He had tried to tell them. When he was first accosted by the precocious child, he hid behind his owner's legs. When this proved to be false sanctuary, because his owner was too preoccupied to notice, he sat under the dining-room table among the chair legs. But Jemima soon had the chairs out and joined him. He sought haven in the garden but was finally forced to retreat to his bed.

No one noticed, no one called off this persistent perisher. When she tried to pick him up, his patience finally snapped, and now he's dead. The moral of this story is obvious: but too late for Jack and the Sweets.

If you feel that your dog finds it difficult to cope with the presence of toddlers and younger children in your home, its response will be made more positive if it knows that it can escape their attentions if it has to. This is due to the fact that your dog can then control its own environment which in turn will reduce its stress. A method of achieving this with small- and medium-sized dogs is to place batons either side of a door that provides access to a room your dog is used to going in to, e.g. to get to its bed, or a place it generally likes to be in. A board that is about the height of a childgate can then be inserted across the gap. In the board there should be a dog flap so that your dog can go backwards and forwards as it wishes, but you will have the option of locking the flap if necessary. Adult members of the household will be able to step over the board, and it will be easier to tell if children are about to invade your dog's haven and distract them than if the barrier did not exist. Some owners use their dog's bed, indoor kennel or a room without the use of a barrier as the place it can go to for safety. This is less effective because it is not as obvious to the dog that there is a line across which the children cannot cross.

As already stated, you will only have to consider the method described above if you feel that your dog is stressed by the presence of children. The majority of dogs continue to integrate well with the family as it grows with no difficulty. However this should not lead us into complacency. If dogs are pushed too far they will react. What can be unpredictable to both dog and parent is the behaviour of the child. As a consequence of this dogs and children should never be left together unattended. When they are together and supervised the children should be prevented from treating the dog as if it has boundless tolerance. There is a danger that the more a child is told to leave the dog alone the more it will torment it as a means of getting attention. This can be prevented by distracting the child and giving it attention when it is behaving appropriately, (by the time you finish this book this will sound familiar) and, once it is old enough to understand, rewarding it for leaving the dog alone.

Boarding Kennels

When you go away you may be fortunate enough to stay in an exotic villa, but how do you make sure that Fido gets five star digs?

Many dog owners find themselves contemplating what to do with their pet when holidays approach. Some are able to leave their dog with relatives or friends; some may employ a house-cum-dogsitter, while others arrange their holidays so they can take their dog with them. At some time or another, however, most dog owners are likely to consider the use of boarding kennels.

Many owners regularly board their dogs, safe in the knowledge that their pets are in competent and caring hands. However, some emphatically refuse to use kennels, worried that their dog will be unhappy away from them and its normal surroundings. Despite what these owners think, or like to believe, most dogs adapt to kennel life and their owners' absence very easily.

Much is written about the importance of finding good kennels, and quite rightly so, but the emphasis should not be on the kennels alone. If a dog is to settle, remain unstressed, and come out of the kennels looking happy and in good condition, the owner's preparation for the dog's stay is just as important.

A kennel owner's nightmare scenario is likely to be a dog totally unfamiliar with kennel life and unable to cope if its owners nip to the corner shop, let alone leave it for any greater length of time. Such a dog is likely to be stressed if put in kennels and may lose condition or bark until it is hoarse, with the kennels unjustly getting the blame.

Emphasis should be put on preparing your dog to be able to cope with a stay in kennels. For many the idea of this preparation may appear irrelevant because they have no intention of using kennels. However, you can never tell what unexpected event is around the next corner; a stay in hospital, a spell away to look after a sick relative, the offer of a break which can't be refused or a change in circumstances which may mean the people who normally look after your dog can't have it. In any eventuality, knowing you have the option of putting your dog into kennels, safe in the knowledge that he or she will be happy, can be invaluable, unless you are prepared to employ dog-sitters who will stay in your house when you are away.

Ideally, young dogs should spend a little time in kennels every so often as they grow up. This ensures that they learn to regard the place as their second home. The stay can be during the daytime only to start with, building up to the occasional overnight stay. Although this approach is recommended for young dogs, to ensure the best possible adaptation to a kennel environment, it is also helpful if you have an older dog and intend to board it for the first time. A few overnight or short stays before its first long period in kennels will not only help your dog to become accustomed, it will also allow you to be assured that your dog will be happy in kennels, and you can enjoy your holiday without fretting.

Whether or not your dog is used to a stay in kennels, there are some things you can do to ensure it settles quickly after you have left it. Not least of these is the avoidance of a dramatic last goodbye, so there is less contrast when your presence is withdrawn. A dog that has entered the kennel's reception area quite confidently can soon change its demeanour if the owner is distressed and reluctant to leave, so it is much better to adopt a matter-of-fact attitude for your dog to pick up on.

Ask if you can provide your dog's own bedding and perhaps its favourite toys and chews. These things can help to bridge the gap between kennels and home, and provide a sense of security. If your dog is used to being given two meals a day, you should ask for the kennels to arrange for this to continue in your absence and, as far as possible, the same type of food should be fed. Not only will this continuation of routines help avoid stress, but feeding the same food will help prevent digestive upsets.

You should choose the kennels with care. The personal recommendation of other dog owners is a good guide, but do not rely on other people's recommendations alone. It is a good idea to visit a few kennels to inspect them. This will enable you to make comparisons and determine good from bad. If you own a nervous dog or one unused to kennels, it may settle better in a smaller establishment where there is less noise and general activity.

All boarding kennels should have a licence from the local authority, but this tells you more about cleanliness and housing standards than about how knowledgeable or caring the proprietors and their staff are. To help you make some assessment about these aspects, arrange a tour of the kennels before you book your dog in. It is a good idea to engage the owners and staff in conversation. This will enable you to determine whether you are comfortable with the thought of them looking after your faithful companion.

During your visit, check if the kennels look clean and tidy and the dogs in them look content. Make sure you ask to see all the kennels on the site, just in case the proprietor is tempted to show you the newest block while avoiding others that you may not be so happy with. If your dog has a tendency to bark at other dogs when you walk it on a lead, ensure it is not housed where it has the chance to bark at a procession of dogs that are walked backwards and forwards in front of its kennel, otherwise you could come home to find the problem is much worse.

NOTES

1.   Wickens, S. *Lecture on Dominance: How does it develop and how do people fit in* Given at the Association of Pet Behaviour Councilors Symposium 1994 presented by Bradshaw, J. (published in APBC proceedings 1994)

2.   McBride, E.A., Bradshaw, J.W.S., Christians, A. McPhearson, J. and Bailey, G. *'Factors Pre-disposing Dogs to Separation Problems'* Proceedings of the 29th International Congress of the International Society for Applied Ethology ed. by Rutter, Rushen, Randle and Eddison (University Federation for Animal Welfare 1995)

3.   Serpell, J.A. & Jagoe, A. *'Early Experience and the Development of Behaviour'* The Domestic Dog: Its Evolution, Behaviour and Interactions with People ed. Serpell, J.A. (Cambridge University Press 1995)

—— 4. ——

Talking To Your Dog

When we communicate with other people we do not just use verbal language. Communication also includes body language, vocal intonation and facial expression, and can be intentional or subconscious. One of the things man and dog have in common is an ability to use language to maintain the social structure, and to an extent both languages are similar. For example, standing tall tends to indicate confidence in both species, while reducing height implies apprehension or submission.

Dogs and people are descendants of individual creatures which developed the capacity to use language to avoid conflict with others of their kind, and consequently lived together as a cohesive unit. Interestingly, the fox, which has not evolved to be a pack animal, does not have such an extensive repertoire of facial and body language as that found in both the dog and the wolf.

However, dogs are not born communicators; but they do inherit the ability to learn communication skills. The experiment already discussed on page 25 helps to illustrate this point. Three groups of puppies were kept in isolation from each other.

- One group had contact only with humans
- The second group had an equal amount of exposure to humans and to other dogs
- The third group only had the opportunity to interact with other puppies.

When the three groups were finally brought together, it was found that the puppies tended to stay together in these groups. What was it that the puppies saw in each other that encouraged them to maintain these distinct social groups? Unless each group smelt different, the selection process must have been the result of some variation in the way they communicated.

Learning the lingo

The capacity for humans and dogs to communicate with their own kind and each other normally helps the two species to live together in harmony, but we can be guilty both of giving off the wrong signals and of misinterpreting our dogs. However, misunderstandings or injustices can be avoided if we take the trouble to communicate effectively and read our dog's language properly. Dogs learn how to react to our body language (facial expressions etc.), and we should take the time to develop our communication skills with them. It is generally accepted that the way to do this is by emulating the dog's own language. Obviously we lack the full repertoire of canine communication attributes, such as hackles and a tail. But we do have, for example, the ability to draw ourselves up to our full height and fix a dog with a threatening stare if we need to convey annoyance or a threat. (This is a potentially provocative action, though, because it intimidates the dog, and it should be used with circumspection.)

The language a dog responds to can be extremely subtle. Just looking at your dog can be enough to encourage it to carry on doing something because it finds your attention rewarding. This is useful if you want your dog to do whatever it is that it is doing, but counter-productive if you want it to stop. If, for instance, a young dog is having a "mad half hour" and charging about a room, then the more its owners look at it, the more the behaviour is reinforced. Similarly, if a dog is in the habit of running to a window and barking at everything that happens outside, and the owners look up from what they are doing and focus their attention on their dog, it is possible that the look will be taken as a reward and cause the behaviour to be repeated. One of the ways you can tell whether or not this learning process has occurred is to observe your dog when it does something you do not want it to do. If you find that it intermittently looks to see if you are watching, you can be fairly certain that your response to its behaviour has been rewarding it in the past and encourages it to repeat the action.

Rather than considering a part of a dog's body or other language in isolation, it is important to look at a dog's whole demeanour. For example, the baring of teeth can be associated both with threatening and appeasement behaviour. Furthermore, man has changed the

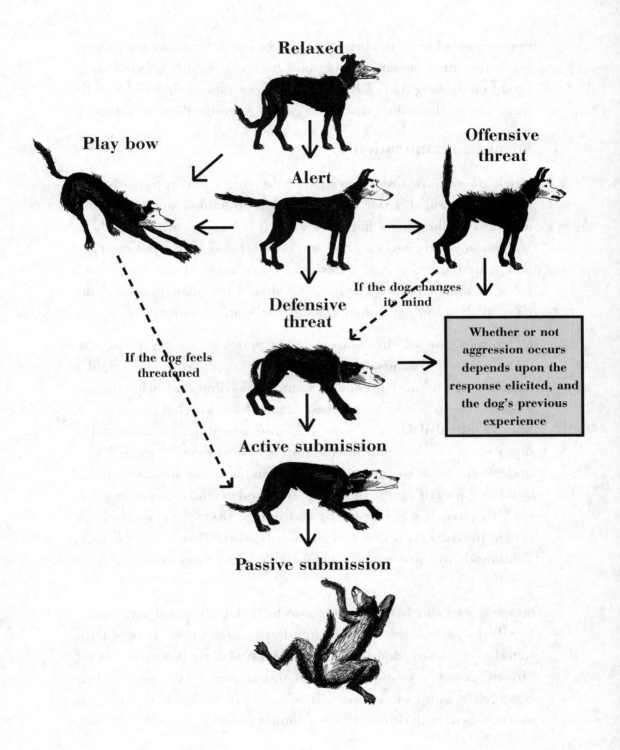

Relaxed

Play bow

Alert

Offensive threat

Defensive threat

If the dog changes its mind

If the dog feels threatened

Whether or not aggression occurs depends upon the response elicited, and the dog's previous experience

Active submission

Passive submission

appearance of so many breeds (often for cosmetic reasons), with the result that their signalling repertoire has been greatly affected. Dogs bred to have long hair, for example, cannot raise their hackles in the same way as those dogs that more closely resemble their ancestors.

Vocal Communication

Much of our misunderstanding of the dog's perception of vocal language is probably due to our exposure to animal stories. We have all willed on the canine film hero when it has been sent to fetch help. Without any conscious effort we suspend disbelief for the duration and accept that the dog has understood every word of the instructions given by the supporting cast, but we should not allow this entertainment to affect our perception of an animal's abilities in the real world.

Of course one of the reasons why many of us have dogs as companions is because we like to natter to them as we would a friend, and why not? It enhances our relationship and helps the dog fulfil its role in society as our best friend. Idle chit chat is one thing. Speech intended for a specific response is a different matter. But many of us walk straight into the trap of talking to our dogs as if they understand what we are saying. How many times have you heard family or friends claim that their dog understands everything they say? In part this is caused by the notion that dogs comprehend simple instructions because of the words used. This is not the case. Commands are just sounds which dogs learn to associate with an action.

Suppose your dog has been taught to lie down when you say 'down'. It will do so because it understands the association between the sound of the word 'down' and the position of lying down. If you say 'drown' however your dog will not throw itself in the nearest lake clutching a lump of concrete. It will simply lie down because the words 'down' and 'drown' make a similar sound.

Although dogs do not understand verbal definitions per se we must not use words indiscriminately, because to do so will give the wrong signals and lead to confusion. Consider the dog that has been trained to lie down when it hears the sound 'down'. On being found lying on some furniture and told to 'get down', it cannot be blamed for not moving, because it was lying down when it received the signal. Another signal must be used to make the dog remove itself.

This little tale illustrates why we need to use words carefully.

Misdirections

Mr Frank sits in his armchair in front of a log fire watching his favourite sport on the television, when Bruno, the family's Boxer, appears in the hall doorway. Bruno, an excitable dog at the best of times, has just returned from a walk with Mrs Frank and is covered up to his elbows in mud. To protect the carpets Mr Frank tries to get Bruno out of the hall and back into the kitchen as fast as possible.

"Bruno!" he exclaims.

This sound means 'come to me'; so Bruno promptly pads a trail of foot prints towards Mr Frank, who screams

"No! Out, Bruno!"

Bruno stops in his tracks at the words 'no' and 'out', but hearing his name he again moves sheepishly towards Mr Frank, who by now is losing his temper.

"Bruno!" he shouts.

Bruno tilts his head to one side; then, concerned at his owner's aggressive behaviour, he starts to cower.

71

"Bruno!" screams Mr Frank, now totally frustrated at not being able to get a response.

Bruno is now so stressed by the situation that he jumps up and attempts to show submission by licking Mr Frank's angry face. Mr Frank, now adorned with two large muddy paw marks on his shirt, really flips his lid.

"Down!" he yells.

Bruno drops to the floor with a thud. Mr Frank, alarmed at the fact that more mud has just been dropped onto the carpet, yells

"Get Out!"

Bruno recognises the signal 'out' and promptly heads for the door. As he watches Bruno retreating, Mr Frank can't resist firing off one last exclamation.

"You're a bad boy", he growls through clenched teeth.

Bruno stops in his tracks. He'd got it right, he was heading towards the door but now his owner is giving off aggressive signals which means more trouble, so with a sigh Bruno flops on the floor submissively, splattering mud everywhere. Mr Frank's reaction is spectacular and it is accompanied by the most interesting language.

Mrs Frank, who has been removing her outdoor clothes, puts her head round the door to see what all the commotion is about. The sight that greets her is shocking. The carpet is covered with paw prints. Bruno has rolled onto his back in a further display of submission which the purple-faced Mr Frank clearly believes is defiance and is now attempting to punish.

"This dog is stupid!" he splutters.

Mrs Frank clicks her fingers and says "Kitchen!" which she promptly backs up by pointing in the appropriate direction. Bruno recognises these signals and in an instant he leaps to his feet and heads into the hall

"Good boy," Mrs. Frank says automatically, and Bruno, sure of what is required, pads into the kitchen.

Mr Frank flops into his chair, muttering "That dog's got a mind of its own. One word from me and he does just what he wants."

It's not what you say, it's the way that you say it

A dog's repertoire of sounds includes grunting, whining, yelping, screaming, howling, growling, tooth snapping; panting as a form of play soliciting; and a type of cough that is sometimes used in defence, and sometimes as a threat.

These sounds may be expressed differently to communicate different things. You may think that a bark is a bark; however, depending on its intonation a bark can indicate: a greeting; play soliciting; defensiveness; threat; care seeking; distress or pain; seeking contact with others; and it can be used as a communal activity.

The fact that dogs communicate a variety of things to each other by altering the tone of their bark, whine, yap etc. should make us sensitive to how dogs perceive our tone of voice. For example, there is no point saying 'good dog' to your dog in deadpan style when it does what is asked. To be effective you should praise your dog enthusiastically, and get its tail wagging. As a rule, if the tail doesn't wag you haven't got the message across. Of course, if your dog has a tendency to get over-excited when it receives praise, you should temper your voice accordingly and give praise in a quiet, soothing manner.

Although changes in tone or inflection may change the message that you are communicating, a change in volume is of less importance. It may be a natural reaction to shout at your dog to stop it from doing something you don't want it to do, such as investigating the contents of a sandwich in your hand; but it is unnecessary. If you get into the habit of shouting at your dog the day may come when it becomes so desensitised that it fails to respond when you most need it to. Generally speaking the only reason for a raised voice is increased distance, although it is worth remembering that a dog's range of hearing is much greater than ours and they can hear over ten times the distance. So it is unnecessary to shout over reasonable distances. It is also unnecessary to bend over to talk to smaller breeds of dog.

In most circumstances it is enough to use the tone of voice you would use with people. If you are trying to encourage someone to do something or praise them you would put an emphasis in your voice to convey your feeling. Similarly you would not have to shout at someone to let them know that you are not very happy about them stealing the food from your plate; the gruff tone of your voice should be enough.

Sight and hand signals

Dogs can distinguish colours, but this is believed to be of limited use because the colours appear pale.[1] This is due to the arrangement of the receptors in the dog's eye, an arrangement which in turn prevents dogs from seeing detail to the same degree as the human eye.[2] If you stand within a group of friends of the same size your dog will seek you out with its nose rather with eyesight. However, your dog can distinguish movement very well over great distances. It is therefore possible to use hand signals for communication, and this is discussed further in chapter 5. It also makes sense to move your arms when you call your dog, so that it can pick you out of the landscape more easily, and distinguish you from other people.

Although shouting commands to your dog is unnecessary, there are times when a note of panic in your voice is unavoidable. If your dog is only used to hearing you use a calm voice, the day that you panic - perhaps because you think your dog will chase a cat, or is running towards the road - it may fail to recognise your signal, and fail to respond. To overcome this practise using a panicky voice from time to time, so that your dog will become accustomed to it, and respond to the signal in all situations.

Misinterpretations

You might think that because dogs can communicate quite effectively without the use of words, we could grasp their language very quickly. Unfortunately this is not the case. Let me give an example.

A parent becomes anxious because the dog growls at his toddling child. Often the dog is trying to indicate that it is unhappy about the presence of the newly mobile child because it is unfamiliar with this phenomenon, owing to its inadequate socialisation in early life. The parent's lack of understanding results in a punitive response, which simply makes the dog more anxious and more inclined to growl. Now you may be thinking to yourself, "Yes, but growling at toddlers is an evil that must be stamped out or, at least, jumped on."

This of course, is not the dog's perspective of the situation. If a dog is pestered by a puppy, the odd growl to show a desire to be left alone would probably be quite effective in deflecting its attentions, especially once the puppy has learnt that a warning growl is followed by a more forceful rebuff if it is not heeded. It is not the dog's fault that a toddler fails to understand and heed the warning. On the other hand, toddlers are unable to understand when dogs are feeling threatened and unable to move out of the way quickly if the dog gives a warning snap.

It is up to parents to compensate for this communication deficit by controlling their toddler's and older children's movements, and preventing them from pestering, climbing on or pulling their dog around. This may seem to be common sense, but it is surprising how many people believe that a dog should put up with all their child's attentions, however unreasonable these attentions may be. (Also see Dogs and Children, p. 56)

One sad incident I came across involved a German Shepherd Dog that was taken to the vet to be put down because it had bitten the owner's child. The vet had always thought that this dog had a good temperament, and he was apparently quite distressed to think that it had bitten someone for no apparent reason. He asked permission to investigate further once the dog had been put to sleep and found, deep within an ear canal, the end of a child's crayon.

Not Guilty

It is not only young children who fail to interpret properly what dogs are communicating. "He knows he has done wrong!" is a claim that owners frequently make. The statement is normally made because at a time when the owners were angry, their dog slunk across the floor, tail clamped between its legs, ears flat against its lowered head and eyes averted from the owner's penetrating stare. In fact the dog has not looked guilty at all. It has looked submissive. Guilt is only possible if there exists a sense of right and wrong and an ability to associate past behaviour with its present results. These are abilities that only humans have.

Although dogs have no abstract notions of history and morals, they do have the capacity to interpret their owner's body language. Armed with this they can recognise when their owners are behaving in an aggressive fashion and respond submissively.

Submissive displays have evolved in our own and canine society as a means of inhibiting aggression in an individual of known greater strength if it attempts to assert itself and impose its will. So it is not surprising that dogs readily adopt a submissive body posture when their owners look annoyed. If this behaviour is interpreted by the owner as guilt it can encourage them to perpetuate the habit of punishing their dog after the event. A reason why submissive behaviour is easily mistaken for guilt is the fact that dogs can learn to anticipate the circumstances in which their owners will behave aggressively i.e. tell them off after the fact. From the owner's perspective it seems as if their dogs look 'guilty' before they have had a chance to see what is wrong.

A woman once told me an anecdote that helps to illustrate the point. She was in the habit of allowing her three dogs to sleep in the bedroom and every morning they would rush downstairs with her. However on the morning in question, she got to the top of the stairs and thought it strange that the dogs had stayed in the bedroom. When she got to the hall she found out why. There, on the hall carpet, was a pile of dog excreta. If dogs had the ability to be guilty one of the three would have stayed upstairs, while the others followed their owner downstairs. It would seem that all three dogs smelt the excreta and decided to stay where they were, out of harm's way. On another occasion I was asked by some clients to help them stop their Staffordshire Bull Terrier bitch, Alice, from urinating in the house. I called at their home and was given a display - in fact, several displays - of the problem. As we entered the owner's living-room, their nine month old bitch ran towards us displaying very submissive behaviour. As she reached our feet she rolled onto her back and squirted a little fountain of urine onto the carpet.

"There you are!" the owners exclaimed; "She does that all the time."

Alice had displayed this behaviour since her owners obtained her at a few weeks of age. Initially she would only do it when her owners bent over her to stroke her, but at the time I saw them they only had to enter the room and she would roll over and do it. Alice was displaying a pattern of submissive behaviour that originates when the puppy's dam licks her blind, deaf and relativity immobile offspring to cause them to defecate and urinate. As the puppies develop and become independently mobile they are able to leave the nest and relieve themselves in a more suitable location. However the act of rolling over and releasing urine remains as a submissive gesture that inhibits aggression in an individual that is a potential threat.

Alice's behaviour became problematical because when she was little she urinated when her owners were looming over her. Their response was to tell her off for soiling the carpet. Although the rebuke was only mild, Alice's sensitivity meant that she was affected by the mildly aggressive display. Of course aggression from these people, who were still looming over her, could only have one result; she rolled over and did it again. This apparent act of defiance did not please the owners, so they told her off again, in response to which she rolled over and again squirted urine, and so on until they only had to enter the room and she would do it.

What I asked the owners to do was enter the room and convey body language that was not threatening. This required them to crouch down on their haunches, with their hands and knees in an open posture. On seeing this Alice approached them, but as she got close she started to roll onto her back as before. The owners stood up and turned their backs to her before she had a chance to squirt urine or even finish rolling. The procedure was repeated many times in the next half an hour, by the end of which Alice did not bother to roll over or squirt urine, because it was no longer an effective means of communicating. Each time she decided not to roll her owners produced titbits from their pockets and gave them to her. Once Alice had learnt that her submissive displays were unnecessary and that not rolling over was rewarded with titbits, she was cured.

The sobering point to this tale is that the owner's opening words on my arrival were to the effect that if I could not cure Alice they would either find a home for her or put her to sleep, and all because they had not seen the situation from her point of view.

Dominance and Submission

Although dogs will roll onto their backs to indicate submission, confident dogs, with no need to show submissive behaviour, will also roll onto their side or backs in some circumstances, such as when encouraging an apprehensive individual to play. Perhaps the body posture says more about not intending to be a threat than simply being a submissive signal. As with Alice's owners we can emulate this action by dropping to our haunches and opening up our hands to convey an open posture. Of course reducing our height also means that we are doing the opposite to indicating a threat. The squatting body posture probably has further significance to dogs, because they learn in puppyhood that people who squat down to their height, which we tend to do out of necessity, are likely to be friendly.

Try squatting down in front of your own dog without any other form of communication and observe whether or not it comes up to you. Other experiments you can try are:

- Lying down on your back when your dog is least expecting it and in locations in which it is not used to seeing it
- Copying the canine rear-end-up head-down play bow in an excited fashion and see if your dog wants to play, or just thinks you've gone mad.

79

Squatting on your haunches is different to bending forward and looming over your dog. Leaning over can be quite threatening and can cause a dog to avoid coming right up to you. Imagine this situation from the dog's point of view. A dominant dog will tower over one of equal size that is adopting a lower and more submissive body posture, and so humans towering over dogs in a similar manner can appear threatening. In some cases this can be made worse if the person tries to catch hold of the dog's collar, in response to which dogs sometimes give a threatening growl or may even give a warning snap.

Do Not Smack or Shake by the Scruff of the Neck

Dogs may be more inclined to snap at hands if they have been smacked in the past. This is something outside the canine repertoire of communication tools; dogs are unable to hit each other, and it is asking a lot to expect them to have to discriminate between a hand raised in anger and one attempting to stroke it or examine it. They can discriminate by observing the other clues in our behaviour, but there is always the chance that they will make a mistake. You can spot the dog that has suffered the indignity of smacking by raising your hand sharply before stroking it. Where smacking has occurred, the raising of the hand is likely to cause the dog to flinch in apprehension. This apprehension can be particularly worrying in situations where children approach dogs and attempt to stroke them. If a dog is already uncertain about how to read the actions of children, and if it has experienced being smacked, it may be inclined to snap at the hand a child extends towards it.

If your dog shows any apprehension about hands it can be cured by repeatedly raising your hand and bringing it down slowly to stroke your dog. You can add to the effect by giving a titbit. If raising your hand in this manner is likely to cause defensive behaviour, rather than cause your dog to flinch or shy away, you should consider asking your vet to refer you to someone who can help, such as a member of the Association of Pet Behaviour Counsellors.

Puppies can be proofed against apprehension about hands by being handled in a kindly way as much as possible in early life. As a result of this they will learn that hands raised towards them from any direction are not a threat, and they will always anticipate pleasant contact.

Owners are sometimes advised that they can discipline their dogs by taking hold of the scruff of the neck, or either side of the neck, and staring into the dog's face while rebuking it. The owners have even been told that this is what the mother dog would do. While a bitch might bowl a puppy over and gently put her mouth on its neck, she obviously cannot possibly imitate the rest of this threatening and frightening human behaviour, which would greatly distress the dog.

A muzzle hold

If you ever feel the need to get physical with your dog, perhaps because you want to reinforce your position as 'pack leader', put your hand *gently*, like a mouth, over its neck, when it is on the ground. This simulates a canine putdown. A muzzle hold can also be used. Another dog would use its mouth, but you can *gently* place your hand around the dog's muzzle for a moment.

Greeting Behaviour

When adult wolves return to the den from a hunting expedition, the cubs that have been left behind will rush up and lick at their muzzles. This stimulates the adults to regurgitate food for the cubs to consume, a sort of 'meals on paws' service for infants. When the cubs grow up they start to accompany the adults on the hunts but muzzle-licking is retained as a gesture. Typically dogs display it on meeting a dominant individual as a form of greeting and appeasement which inhibits aggression.

A puppy in a domestic environment tries, in the same way as its wild cousin, to lick the faces of visitors and the human members of its pack, especially if they have been absent for a while. It isn't possible to reach their faces, so in the attempt it is likely to jump up and may even become vocal out of frustration. Of course, the person is unaware that the puppy wants them to regurgitate their dinner on the hall carpet! To them the attention the puppy gives them is positive proof that it loves them and they greet it with enthusiasm - which, in turn, encourages the puppy to be more demonstrative next time. In this way the puppy can inadvertently be taught to greet people boisterously - especially visitors, who find they cannot resist that 'cute little face' and give the puppy lots of fuss as it bounces around them. As the puppy grows older and puts on a few pounds, its greeting becomes inconvenient. Jumping up can cause the elderly to become alarmed and mothers fearful for their children's safety.

As the list of general embarrassment, laddered stockings and spoilt clothes starts to lengthen, the owners may become frantic in their attempts to control their dog. However, unless it is well-trained and has learnt to respond well, the dog may interpret commands of 'SIT!', screams of 'NO!' and yells of 'BAD DOG!' as their owner's own excitable response to the arrival of the visitor, and because the rest of the pack is getting excited, it may jump up and yap all the more. Eventually the whole scene can become a pantomime that is enacted every time someone enters the home. Some of the misguided remedies sometimes advocated include kneeing the friendly dog in the chest or treading on its back paws as it jumps up. These unnecessarily harsh approaches often cause the problem to get worse. Elderly visitors, for instance, may not be well equipped or willing to conduct these wrestling techniques, and inept attempts are likely to make the dog more excited. Even if the technique is 'effective', there is a chance that the dog will associate the visitor with pain and will consequently feel obliged to show submission when they next call. If so, it may do this by jumping up to lick their face..... and a vicious circle can develop. In the worst case scenario, any pain could cause a dog to become frightened of visitors. (For what to do in these situations see Chapter 5)

Distress not Defiance

People sometimes come into conflict with their dog because they wrongly interpret its behaviour as defiant when it is really being apprehensive. By punishing what they see as a challenge, they unwittingly add fuel to the fire. There are many scenarios in which this can occur. The area of conflict might involve the owner's attempts to get their dog off the furniture, or to move it from one room to another or out of their way. Their dog may not properly interpret the owner's wishes, and may fail to move. This apparent refusal to co-operate may cause the owner to resort to punishment, and in turn this may cause the dog to flatten itself closer to the floor or chair to further indicate submission rather than move. If pushed the dog may even growl defensively making the owner angry and then of course, the problem gets worse. This is an example of the sort of problems that can occur.

The rather less than even-tempered Mrs Wellard is preparing to pop next door.

"Get into the kitchen," she tells her dog.

Normally Mrs Wellard puts her best shoes on if she prepares to go out without him at this time of day, which gives her dog a clue as to what she wants; he will then trot to the kitchen. On this occasion she has not bothered with her shoes and without the clue he fails to respond, because Mrs Wellard has not taught him what responses she wants to her signals, and he has always had to work it out through trial and error. Mrs Wellard draws herself up to her full height.

"Get into the kitchen!" she growls.

The dog has seen this aggression many times before. In anticipation of what is to come, he lowers his body and turns his head and eyes away from her in submission. As she is unschooled in dog language, Mrs Wellard fails to understand the real meaning of what her dog is doing.

"Don't you defy me!" she screams.

Frozen to the spot, in case any movement provokes her to lash out, the dog growls defensively. Mrs Wellard sees this as flagrant disobedience and dislodges him with her foot. The dog gives a warning snap and runs into the kitchen. As he dashes away his rump is stung by Mrs Wellard's hand, who is convinced he knew what was required all the time.

Mrs Wellard is concerned that the dog might be a risk to her children because his snapping is becoming more frequent, and she will talk to her husband about taking him to the rescue society, even though she loves him dearly.

We can avoid situations of this type if we are sensitive to the signals our dogs display, and interpret them properly as events develop. Your dog may roll on its back with its feet in the air as a gesture of submission, but the signal is more likely to be subtle. It may lower its head and body and look away to avoid eye contact. Its tongue may be projected from the front of its mouth in an attitude of licking. This gesture originated as the muzzle licking described above, but does not have to be displayed in the immediate vicinity of the intended recipient's muzzle to be a gesture of appeasement. The action is normally very brief and in many situations you will have to be observant to spot it.

Language and Emotion

Interestingly this tongue projection, crouching and other behaviour has been recorded by some researchers as revealing a measure of the dog's own stress, and is not necessarily triggered in response to aggressive displays from another person or dog. It is interesting to speculate whether submissive body language is in fact the dog's behavioural response to its own emotional state of fear or anxiety, and other dogs learn that he poses no threat to them. This in turn defuses their own potential aggression.

So what should you do if you see your dog slinking across the floor and/or flashing the lick signal at you at a time when:

- you are angry
- your dog anticipates that you might be angry
- your dog misunderstands you and thinks that you are confronting it?

85

Obviously what you should not do is succumb to the temptation to tell it off. What you should do if your dog has done something you did not want it to do, is to remove the cause of the problem. Say, for example, your dog is repeatedly destructive or loses toilet control when it is separated from you. You must either address the cause of its anxiety about your absence, or correct its faulty learning through education. If your dog shrinks in size and/or flashes its tongue at you when you tell it to move from where it has chosen to lie, don't view its lack of response as a defiant act. Ask yourself a few questions.

Has your dog been taught to understand the signals you are using?

Are you expecting it to understand your intentions intuitively?

To overcome the problem remember the circumstances in which the incident occurs and teach your dog what you want it to do, using rewards to reinforce compliant behaviour. In time your dog should become increasingly willing and able to respond to your requests. We will look at many of these aspects throughout the rest of this book.

NOTES

1.   Burton, R. Animal Senses (David and Charles, Newton Abbot, England 1970)
2.   Messant, P. Understanding Your Dog (Macdonald and Jane's Publishers Ltd. 1979)

— 5. —

How Dogs Learn

In order to be able to get the best results when training our dogs, it helps to understand how they learn. This remains true whatever you are doing: teaching a puppy to relieve itself in an appropriate place; teaching your dog to walk by your side, or to come back when called; or preventing and curing behaviour problems.

The word 'training' can conjure up images of military-style drill halls for dogs in which they are marched up and down and shouted at in

87

sergeant-major fashion. To ensure that we have the right approach and attitude we should think instead of teaching our dogs what we want them to know and do. Some people will tell you that they have not trained their dog to be obedient but that they have taught their dog a trick. But to the dog, both tricks and those things which we consider to be acts of obedience are one and the same thing - and they can all be taught.

We have already looked at one form of learning: **habituation,** where an animal learns to ignore something that is not important to its welfare. Animals can also learn to associate a stimulus with the absence of a significant event, so that when it does become a predictor of something it does not trigger a response. This is called **latent inhibition,** and an example of this occurs during puppy parties held at veterinary practices. The puppies attending learn that the veterinary practice is not threatening; in fact, they have a nice time. If, on a subsequent visit, the vet has to conduct a procedure the dog does not like, it should not put it off entering the clinic because the building and the things associated with it are not predictors of something unpleasant.

Habituation and latent inhibition result in a dog learning not to respond to the things around it, but when we want our dogs to do something we have to develop a response.

Pavlov's Dogs (Classical Conditioning)

In the 1920's the Russian scientist Ivan Pavlov [1] wanted to study enzymes. To achieve this he surgically implanted tubes into the salivary glands of dogs from which he was able to collect samples. Although such a procedure may seem unacceptable to us today, Pavlov's experiment has proved invaluable to our understanding of conditioned responses.

Pavlov intended to feed the dogs, thereby causing them to produce the saliva which would then run into the tubes. However, he found that the dogs started to salivate before the food arrived because they responded to clues that told them the food was on its way, such as the arrival of the researcher responsible for feeding, and the noise/smell of the food being prepared. Realising this, Pavlov experimented by letting the dogs hear the sound of a metronome before the food was given, whilst making sure that there were no other clues to which the dogs could react.

He found that after the sound had preceded the food many times, the dogs would salivate when they heard it, even if the food did not arrive. He also found that he could keep this up indefinitely so long as food sometimes followed the sound. This is the basis of what is called **classical conditioning**, i.e. that a stimulus (in this case a sound) that has no apparent importance in itself becomes significant because it predicts something meaningful will follow and triggers an involuntary action, such as salivation.

We can use classical conditioning techniques to trigger a response over which an animal has no control, including emotional states. For example, if a dog gets excited about going for a walk but it is never taken on the lead, a lead will have no significance and will not trigger excitement if it is produced. However, once a dog has been taken for a walk on a lead a few times, the lead will trigger excitement as soon as it is produced, because the dog can predict the walk. Eventually excitement will occur when the dog is shown the lead even if a walk does not follow.

Classical conditioning is often used when training puppies to associate the action of relieving themselves with a particular place rather than any other place, normally outdoors rather than indoors. Traditionally the approach has been to provide the puppy with lots of newspaper so that there is every likelihood that when it relieves itself, it will do it on the paper. The fact that the sensation of relieving itself and the paper become associated makes it more likely that the paper will trigger toileting behaviour next time the puppy needs to 'go'.

Once the association between the newspaper and the act of defecation is firmly established, the amount of newspaper is gradually reduced, and that which is used is moved progressively nearer to the door and finally into the owner's garden. In this example the newspaper is known as the **conditioned stimulus** and the **conditioned response** is going to the toilet. Once the newspaper has reached the garden, the dog learns a **secondary association** with the presence of grass, so that over a period of time the grass becomes a significant stimulus that causes the puppy to relieve itself and the newspaper is no longer required.

I occasionally meet dogs that toilet in an inappropriate place because they no longer have access to grass and they are reluctant to relieve themselves on concrete. Some dogs, on the other hand, prefer to relieve themselves on concrete because they were conditioned to do so in early life. This conditioning can cause problems for people who have got older puppies from a kennel environment. If the puppy has been conditioned to use a concrete floor or, worse still, a concrete floor in an enclosed place, it can be difficult to convince it that it should not toilet in the kitchen.

Luckily for us, Pavlov also discovered that conditioned responses that have been learned can be unlearned. Having found that the dogs in his experiment had learnt to salivate when they heard a metronome, he then ran further tests in which the sound of the metronome was never followed by food. In time the dogs learnt that the metronome no longer predicted the arrival of food, and the conditioned response of salivation stopped. This process is called **extinction.** Let's look at an example of this in everyday life. People often complain that their dog gets too excited when they produce its lead. One of the ways this can be overcome is to repeatedly put the dog's lead on, but never take it for a walk. In time, the lead will no longer predict a walk and will not cause excitement. Of course this is entirely impractical, because you will have to take the poor dog out eventually! A more useful application of this principle is to put the lead on the dog and and take it into the garden to do some exercises, such as walking to heel, sit, lie down, etc. more often than you take the dog for a walk. The association between the lead and training will become more significant than the lead and going for a walk.

It will help further if, even when you are going to take your dog for a walk, you take it into the garden first to do some training. In this way, your dog may not predict that it is going for a walk until you head for the great outdoors instead of the house. This approach falls down, however, if your dog can pick up on more significant clues from which it can predict it is going for a walk, e.g. the type of clothes you are wearing, the time of day, or the fact that walks always follow breakfast etc. The way an animal responds to a stimulus may still vary, depending on how it feels and on what other things are happening around it. For example, when you produce the lead, your dog is less likely to be excited if it is exhausted or if it can see someone preparing its food. Similarly a puppy will not relieve itself on newspaper just because it is there; the puppy also has to have a need to relieve itself.

Operant Conditioning

Dogs also learn on their own. They will simply do something and find out if the outcome of their behaviour is rewarding or unpleasant.

- If the outcome is pleasant or beneficial, the dog will probably repeat the behaviour. We call this **reinforcement**.

- If the outcome is unpleasant or unrewarding in some way, the dog will probably not do it again. We call this **punishment.**

Although the term 'punishment' is applied here, we should see this as a technical term only.

The classic experiment that shows the principle of this form of learning was conducted by Thorndyke in the early **1900**'s.[2] He put a cat in a box that had a mechanism that allowed the cat to let itself out. Through a process of exploration, the cat stumbled upon the behaviour which released the catch which was rewarded (**reinforced**) by the outcome of getting out. This predisposed the cat to repeat the action more quickly the next time it was put in the box. The more often this happened, the more the learning was established. Eventually the cat would let itself out of the box as soon as it was put in.

Further typical behavioural research[3] might involve a rat running around a featureless box until it happens to press a lever which releases some food for it to eat. After a period of trial and error, the rat learns that pressing the lever produces food. This form of learning is called **operant conditioning** or **instrumental learning.**

For an example of how we can use this form of learning with our dogs, let's return to the example of dogs getting excited when their lead is produced. This excitement can be irritating because the dog's activity makes it difficult to put the lead on. But the owner's irritation and consequent attempts to control the dog may unwittingly reward and therefore reinforce the behaviour. If this happens to you, try this experiment. Get ready to go for a walk as usual and at the appropriate time reach down to put your dog's lead on. When your dog gets excited, stand up straight and move the lead away from its head and neck by drawing it up to your chest, without saying anything. Wait until your dog has settled again and sits expectantly in front of you, while you remain quiet and still. When your dog sits, reach down to put the lead on again. If your dog moves, repeat the action of raising the lead up to your chest. Keep repeating the process and eventually your dog will realise that excitement results in the lead moving further away, rather than going on and the walk starting. As your dog wants the lead on, it will eventually choose to sit quietly to get the reward - the reinforcement - of the lead going on. If you repeat this process every time you put your dog's lead on it will learn to sit in front of you to get what it wants as quickly as possible.

For another example of how we can use operant conditioning let's look at the problem of the dog jumping up when you return home. If your dog finds that its excitable behaviour and jumping up in response to your "Hello!" are ignored, it will continue for a while, but it will eventually stop because its behaviour goes unrewarded (punished, in this case, by the withdrawal of something nice - your attention). If you give attention as soon as your dog sits quietly, sitting will be reinforced; the dog is more likely to sit the next time you enter the house. The more this occurs the sooner your dog will learn that jumping up is pointless, and that sitting is followed by the attention it likes; and it will choose the latter.

You will have to be careful to ensure that your dog is not unwittingly rewarded for jumping up. The main objective of jumping up in this situation is to get a response from you, and what constitutes a response can be very subtle. Even looking at your dog or telling it to stop can be enough to encourage it to continue. When you ask regular visitors to use the same approach, as you should, you will find your dog's behaviour will be very different with those people who ignore your dog until it is settled, than it is with people who are inconsistent or who carry on as before. This is because dogs learn to anticipate the response they are likely to get from each individual and act accordingly. In effect they learn to discriminate between people.

Teaching your dog to sit

Operant Conditioning Using The Lure Reward Technique

You can use operant training to teach your dog exercises, such as sit. Although your dog will probably already sit when asked, it may be useful to do these exercises to become familiar with the approach because the principle can be applied to most things you want to teach your dog.

Sit

- Hold a titbit just above your dog's head and just out of its reach.
- Wait patiently, ignoring everything your dog does, until it sits. (It will probably do this because the food is just above its head and it is looking up. If its head goes up its hind quarters will go down, and there you are. A sitting dog.)
- If necessary you can bring the titbit close to your dog's nose and raise it up slowly so as to **lure** your dog's head upward as it follows your hand.
- When your dog chooses to sit praise it and give it the titbit.

This is called **lure-reward** training.

After a few repetitions your dog will learn to sit to get the titbit (the reinforcer) when you raise your hand without delay. Once you are sure your dog has learnt to sit as quickly as possible to get the titbit you can start to say *'sit'* as soon as your dog starts the action of sitting. In time your dog will learn to discriminate between the sound of the word 'sit' and all the other information it receives from the environment, and associate it with the action it has to perform to get the reward. You can then use the word 'sit' to trigger the action of sitting.

95

Teaching your dog 'down'

Down

To use operant conditioning to teach your dog to lie down:

- Kneel on the floor or sit in a low chair with your dog in front of you

- Hold a titbit between finger and thumb in front of its nose and gradually lower it to floor level. You should be able to lure your dog into almost lying down on the floor, although you may have to guide it down several times with the same piece of food if it keeps sitting up.

- At some point your dog may worry at your hand in an attempt to get the titbit, but do not let go until your dog is flat on the floor.

- Your dog will quickly learn that the way to get the titbit quickly is to lie down as soon as it anticipates what is required.

- At this point you can start to add the discriminating stimulus of the word 'down' so that your dog learns that if it lies down quickly when it hears the word it will get a titbit.

- As soon as it is apparent that your dog has learned to respond to the signal you give it to trigger the action, you should fade out using the lure. Your dog might otherwise become dependent on it. See more on reinforcers on page 98. You can also develop a particular hand movement from these exercises so that your dog will learn to respond to this hand signal, even at a distance.

Sometimes, training a dog to do something is built up in gradual stages, a process called **shaping.** This is discussed more fully in conjunction with Clicker Traing in chapter 10.

When To Start Teaching A Puppy

Traditionally, dog clubs and trainers used to tell owners that their dog would not be ready for serious training until it was six months old. What they meant was: *'your dog will not be able to stand up to the harsh methods we use until it is six months old'*. But with operant training this attitude is unnecessary and puppies can start to learn almost as soon as they can walk. This may seem rather young to some readers; but puppies can learn to sit and lie down and recall for titbits just as easily as an adult. A puppy is a capable creature.

For example, if your puppy follows you to a door it wants to go through, but finds that you just stand there holding the handle it will not know how to behave. On finding its access denied it will try various actions and will eventually sit down. At this point you should open the door. You will not have to repeat this very often before your puppy learns that it can open doors by sitting in front of them. It will also learn to associate the sound of the word 'sit' with the position if you add the word as it starts to perform the action. You can use this method to teach various tricks. For example, most dogs have a strong drive to lift a paw in the air when they want something. This is a food begging action that accompanies the muzzle-licking that wolf cubs display towards adults returning from a hunt; but it is first seen during suckling when pups knead the mammary glands with their paws to stimulate milk flow. If you reward, and therefore reinforce this behaviour when your dog puts its paw on your hand you will make it more likely to happen. Once your dog has learnt to put a paw up when you extend your hand to it, you can add the discriminating stimulus of the word 'paw' to trigger the behaviour.

More on Reinforcers

As we have seen, a reinforcer is anything that is likely to make an action occur more frequently; and there are both positive and negative reinforcers. A simple maxim that helps to remember the meaning of negative reinforcement is: *'It's nice when it stops'*. An example of the application might be to give you a choice of six chairs to sit on and to keep giving you electric shocks until you sit on the right one. You would probably learn where not to sit; but you might consider it a very stressful process.

To decide on what would serve as a positive reinforcer, think about what motivates your dog. The majority of dogs respond well to the praise and affection they receive when they react to a signal such as the words 'come', 'down' or 'sit'.

When you start to train your dog to do something new, praise alone may not be enough of a reinforcer to motivate it to repeat the action. Often it is easier to motivate a dog with other things such as titbit rewards or the production of a toy from a pocket. Do not be concerned that the use of titbits will cause your dog to put on weight. You can deduct the food you use from its daily food allowance. To treat behaviour problems, I often ask owners to feed their dog a dried food, and to use some or all of it as reinforcers for appropriate behaviour. Sadly, there is a resistance to rewarding dogs with food because there is a tradition that still prevails in some quarters that dogs should *'obey through respect'*.

This is shorthand for 'getting a response' because the dog anticipates the displeasure of the owner if it does not do what it is told, and the behaviour that leads to the avoidance of the owners displeasure is the one the dog learns to choose. This is as stressful for the dog as our electric chair example would be for us. We should always remember that excessive stress inhibits learning.

It may be that some people continue to use a punitive approach because of the feeling of power it gives them. Perhaps training that focuses on positive reinforcement even goes against the grain of human nature. We are too quick to feel affronted and to punish our dogs for not obeying. Sea lions, dolphins and even cats can have an amazing repertoire of tricks, but any attempt to use punishment with these, and other species, would send them flying for cover. Sadly for the dog, its pack instinct causes it to come submissively cringing back for more. A more rational, although misguided reason why some people resist the use of material rewards is the belief that it is tantamount to bribery and that you will always be dependent upon them. Certainly, it would be bribery if you stood in the park and waved a titbit in front of your dog or rattled a biscuit tin to encourage it to come back. But apart from during lure-reward training, which is used to establish a behaviour, the reinforcer is not produced until the desired behaviour has been performed. When a behaviour has become firmly established, the use of titbits or toys can gradually be withdrawn and you can just use praise if you want to.

Reinforcing behaviour with praise alone is easier where your dog has not got anything better to do. You may, for example, teach a puppy to jump into the back of your car by luring and reinforcing with titbits, but when it has learnt to do it on request you will no longer need to use food, not least because most dogs like to get into the car because they find car journeys exciting. However, you may want to carry on using titbits as reinforcers if your dog is apprehensive about getting in your car (see Chapter 13), or if it is reluctant to get in at the end of a walk.

If your dog is surrounded by exciting reasons to do something other than what you want it do, it may be a good idea to keep using material rewards after a behaviour has been established. For example, you may teach your dog to come to you when you call it (see page 148) but in a park there may be distractions present, such as other dogs, that motivate it to do something else. Rewards may help it focus on coming back to you.

Intermittent Rewards

If you reward your dog with a titbit every time it returns to you however long it takes to return, it will learn that it can investigate all the tempting smells around, etc., before sauntering back in its own time and still get the reward. To prevent this, be selective.

When your dog has learnt to come back for a titbit, switch to rewarding the very best responses, which will result in faster recalls. When your dog's recalls are all of lightning speed, switch from rewarding good recalls constantly, to rewarding intermittently.

Intermittent rewards are a powerful way to manipulate behaviour. In fact, for the recipient, they can become addictive. This is the underlying principle behind gambling that causes some people to become compulsive. They are convinced, by the wins they get every so often, that they will win again if they keep working at it and the next one may be the big one. If you think you are immune to this phenomenon, remember that the National Lottery has thousands of £10 prizes every week, so either you or someone you know wins every so often, just to keep people at it. Just in case the next one is the big one.

To develop the best responses in your dog, reward it randomly sometimes after three recalls, sometimes after five, and so on. When it does something especially well, increase the amount of reward. The power of intermittent reinforcers can be applied to all aspects of teaching your dog: whether you are teaching it to sit, lie down, walk by your side without pulling, or anything else.

Intermittent reinforcement can, however, also perpetuate unwanted behaviour. Say, for example, you refrain completely from feeding your dog from the table, to stop it from scrounging at meal times.

You will succeed far better than if you were to attempt the same thing but hand something to your dog occasionally. In this case the scrounging behaviour will become worse than before. This is because the dog tries harder, convinced that if it keeps working at it, it will eventually be successful again.

Something for nothing

So far I have concentrated on the subject of rewarding your dog's response to your signals and wishes, but on many occasions a dog should be rewarded for doing nothing. If you find that difficult to believe, think how many times you would be grateful if your dog did not react to something or to a particular situation. If you are one of the lucky people whose dog does not over-react to things, think how you would feel if they started to. For example, just think how sick you would feel if your loving Fido landed you in court because it snapped at a child that dashed past while you were walking together.

It is, of course, much easier to recognise the presence of an undesirable trait than the absence of one, and we all have a tendency to ignore our dogs when they behave in a manner we find convenient. If you think about it, you can probably come up with many situations where you should praise your dog for doing nothing, rather than ignoring it, because its behaviour is convenient. Next time it does not snap, pull towards other dogs, bark when travelling in your car etc., show your dog some gratitude, and at the same time do yourself a favour by rewarding and therefore reinforcing appropriate behaviour.

The timing of rewards

Always remember the important principle that rewards should be given at the time your dog does what you want. There is no point in giving your dog a reward when you get home, because it did not pull on the lead when you were on the walk. The rewards must be at the time your dog walks the way you want it to, because its capacity to associate a behaviour and its outcome is limited to half a second.

Punishment

Some forms of behaviour have to be to inhibited because they are dangerous, or the consequences are too severe or too costly to tolerate. For example, if a large boisterous dog keeps jumping up at its owner's elderly mother, she could end up being badly hurt. Ignoring the dog until it chooses to sit may not be an option because of the risks in the meantime.

Ideally, the dog's appropriate behaviour should be established before the elderly lady meets the dog, but this may not be possible. The dog should be kept on a lead until it has got over its initial excitement. This will stop the dog from jumping up, providing plenty of opportunity to reward the dog for not doing it. But perhaps the dog is too strong for you to hold, or keeping it on a lead simply frustrates it causing it to bark. In this case you may have to use an alternative approach.

As we have seen in the previous chapter, **punishment** is a technical term for an action that reduces the likelihood of a behaviour being repeated. It does not necessarily imply physical punishment. Unfortunately the word 'punishment' suggests that dogs understand the difference between right and wrong.

Unwanted actions can be inhibited by associating them with an **unpleasant experience,** and the best deterrents are achieved by making the dog's own actions counter productive. For example, if the dog dislikes water, granny can be armed with a water pistol! Every time the dog attempts to jump up, she can surreptitiously squirt it. She must be surreptitious about it, however; otherwise the dog may associate the arrival of the water as her response to it jumping up, and find this rewarding enough to suffer the water.

If this proves to be the case with your dog, you could try using the deterrent spray 'Bitter Apple', or 'Down Dog' . These taste and smell unpleasant and come in pump-action bottles. As with the water, they should be used in a surreptitious manner so that the release of the smell by the visitor appears, to the dog, to be caused by its own behaviour. The effect is normally immediate - rather like going to hug someone who has been eating lots of garlic; you will wish you hadn't done it. When the dog decides to adopt a more appropriate behaviour, such as sitting, that behaviour can be reinforced as discussed above.

Some behaviour is so rewarding in itself that it is vitally important to inhibit it - not least because it can be hard to come up with an alternative as attractive as the behaviour you want to stop. For example, if you find that, when you are watching television, your dog makes its way to your kitchen, jumps up at the work-top and helps itself to what it can find, you will want to stop this behaviour. (See Teaching Your Dog to Leave and Stay - Chapter 8).

Because your dog has the prospect of food, it is difficult to provide a bigger incentive to staying with you than trawling the kitchen. You may be able to control the problem by keeping the surfaces clear, but momentary lapses when your dog can succeed will result in intermittent reinforcement which, as we have already seen, is a powerful incentive for the dog to carry on raiding the kitchen.

Trying to ambush your dog won't work because it will soon learn when it is safe to search the worktops and when it is not. Additionally, if part of your dog's motivation for raiding the kitchen is the attention it gets when you try and stop it, it will stage more raids to stop you watching television etc.

If you do manage to catch your dog in the act and go in with all guns blazing it may seem, from your dog's point of view, that you are competing for something worth having. Your dog will try even harder and get sneaky with it; or, worse still, it could become defensive.

Aversion Tactics

You can try leaving out food that the dog will actively dislike. The use of food filled with mustard, chilli peppers or Tabasco sauce left out for the dog to 'steal' is sometimes advocated. It may work. Then again, the dog might just eat it anyway. Remember that dogs have evolved to be able to digest things that would disgust us. They have relatively little sense of taste and rely much more on their sense of smell. Even if your dog does dislike the taste of chilli, it may learn to discriminate what food to eat and what to leave by sniffing it first.

An alternative form of entrapment involves placing a spring-loaded cap firing trap (available from joke shops) under the only food item left out on the work surface. When your dog moves the potential trophy there is a small 'explosion'. By repeatedly setting this up your dog should learn to view any items of food left on this surface with suspicion, and avoid them.

You could tie a piece of thin string to the food or other item left out for your dog to steal, and attach it at the other end to saucepan lids or tin cans that will fall to the ground as the food is taken. Indeed, you could spend many happy hours devising such booby-traps!

Another tactic to try is the throwing of a check chain at a tin tray. If, for example, you have problems keeping your dog off the furniture when you are present, despite your best efforts, prop a tin tray (one from the pub, not the oven, because the latter type tends to go 'donk' rather than 'bang') against the piece of furniture it likes to get up on to, and wait. Whilst making sure your dog is not looking at you, throw the chain at the tray as the dog is getting up onto the item of furniture. Your dog should leap off. When it looks at you, be busy doing something else, like counting the cracks in the ceiling, so that you don't seem to be involved with the arrival of the bang. After this has happened a few times your dog should suspect that the furniture goes bang when it gets on it, at least when people are in the house, and avoid doing it.

Remote punishment devices

These are available commercially and are increasingly easy to obtain. They come in a variety of shapes and sizes. These range from gas-propelled rape alarms, to electric collars triggered by remote control when the dog barks or when it either steps over a wire or goes between two posts in the garden. The widespread use of electronic devices which deliver electric shocks to dogs for the purpose of 'training' or curing behaviour problems is, in my view, highly undesirable. Their potential for accidental misuse is high and where this occurs they can easily cause unnecessary pain or distress. Electric shocks will be associated with whatever the dog happens to be focused on at the time they arrive, and the wrong association can be made with potentially disastrous results if that happens to be an unrelated object, such as another dog, the owner or a child. Additionally a dog can learn to associate the area in which it receives the shock with the sensation and may try to avoid it in future. Even where a dog learns to associate a shock with a type of unwanted behaviour it may take it some time to work out what it has to do to avoid the shock occurring.

In addition, it is possible for some of these devices to be triggered by external influences, or malfunction, which may result in delivery of shocks not associated with the performance of undesirable behaviour. In the case of those devices that are designed to give a shock or deliver a scented spray when the dog barks, there is no mechanism to discriminate between appropriate and inappropriate barking. Just as importantly, their use encourages the user to suppress the symptoms of a problem without addressing the cause. Those devices that are designed to keep dogs within a boundary would be counter-productive if the dog gets through despite the pain and finds that it gets a shock every time it tries to get back in.

I think that electric collars are only appropriate when the dog's behaviour is life-threatening and all other attempts to modify it have failed, for example when a dog chases sheep. Even then, I think, they should only be used in the hands of an experienced specialist who can determine whether their use is necessary and who is capable of accurate timing. I must point out at this stage however that I have never used an electric collar and that to my knowledge neither have most of my colleagues.

There are various ways by which behaviour can be interrupted, most of which require the use of something aversive to startle the dog or at least arrest its attention for a moment so that the owner can redirect the dog onto another behaviour.

- The use of a water pistol can be effective to start with, but it can be difficult to convince a dog that the user is not involved in the arrival of the water; however nonchalant granny may appear, the dog can still see the pistol in her hand!

- A method that is sometimes advocated[4] is the use of a few pebbles sealed in a soft drinks can which can be thrown so that it lands behind the dog to startle it. The dog can become so conditioned to respond to the sound that it will stop doing the undesirable action if the owner simply rattles the can in his or her hand. This occurs because the dog learns that the can will thud to the ground behind it if it continues to do what it is doing. This is fine as far as it goes, but it is a crude method of conditioning when compared with conditioned avoidance learning.

- The use of Training Discs (five cymbals on a key ring), and of such things as a camera flash gun (useful for deaf dogs) is well established in pet behaviour therapy as **discriminative stimuli for frustrative non-reward** - which is to say, the dog learns to link their use with it not getting something that it might otherwise have expected to get. The discs are effective because, as far as the dog is concerned, they are a novel stimulus and the introduction process to conditioned avoidance learning, which links the dog with a fear of failure.

The normal procedure for introduction of training discs is as follows:

1. Put a piece of food on the floor for your dog. Repeat this. An association develops and the dog expects that your hand moving to the floor will open up when it gets there so that it can have the food.

2. Now, with your Training Discs at the ready, put a piece of food on the floor but retain it between your finger and thumb. As your dog attempts to investigate the food, click the discs in your other hand then throw them to the floor whilst simultaneously withdrawing the food. Your dog will be startled by the absence of the food, but will not initially associate it with the sound of the discs. Once your dog has heard the discs and experienced the fact that the sound is followed by not getting the food it expects a few times, it will avoid the situation either as the hand goes to the floor in anticipation of the sound of the discs and the disappearance of the food, or as soon as it hears the discs. This is because the sound of the discs warns it that it is going to fail to get the food it expects to get, which worries the dog. Typically a dog will choose to sit by another member of the family or under their chair to seek a sense of security. By praising the dog for adopting this avoidance response you will predispose it to an avoidance response when it hears the sound of the discs on subsequent occasions.

3. After successful introduction, the discs can be used to cause the dog to avoid other behaviour such as aggression, jumping up etc.

This may all seem a bit far-fetched, but here is an account of the sort of research on which the idea is based[6] :

A rat was placed at one end of a **30** foot runway and food was placed in a goal box at the other end. The rat learnt to run down the runway for the food and with repetition the behaviour became established. As you might expect, when the researchers stopped putting food in the box the rat gradually gave up running it. However this did not indicate how it responded emotionally to the experience of non-reward. Did it stop running to the goal box simply because there was no food there, (**extinction**) or did it avoid it because it

109

wanted to avoid the unpleasantness of not getting a reward ?

A ledge was then placed around the goal box and it was found that rats experienced the non-reward of no food when the box was found to be empty. After having found food in the goal box on the 300 previous occasions, the rats were so startled by the absence of what they expected to find that they jumped onto the ledge to escape.

A further experiment involved training rats on a partial reinforcement schedule. Sometimes there was food in the goal box at the end of a runway and sometimes there was none. On those occasions when the food reward was absent, a light and sound were turned on as the rat entered the goal box. Once the association between light and sound and no food had been established, the rat was placed on one side of a shuttle box (a simple box divided in half by a low wall). The light and sound that had previously been associated with the absence of food were turned on and the rat would jump over the wall to escape and turn the light and sound off. They would jump the wall more reliably than the other rats that had been taught that there was food on the other side of the barrier when the light or sound came on.

For an analogy, imagine that you go to your kitchen door first thing in the morning, as you have been doing for years, only to find that when you open the door the kitchen has gone. You are going to jump. But you are also human and can possibly rationalise what has happened; to an animal there is just the shock of the absence of what it was expecting. To take our surreal kitchen analogy further, imagine that sometimes your kitchen will be where you expect it to be each morning and sometimes it will be missing. On those occasions the kitchen will be missing a buzzer will go off behind you. Eventually you will jump when you hear the buzzer because it warns you to expect the shock of the kitchen's absence when you open the door. If you are a nervous person, the sound of the buzzer might put you off opening the door altogether.

The significance of conditioned avoidance learning is that it can be used to cause a dog to avoid performing other behaviours because it anticipates failure when it hears the sound of the discs. For example, a dog jumping up to get food from a kitchen work surface can be made to jump down and ignore the food on top by the owner clicking the discs then throwing them to the floor.

This will only work however if the dog is still approaching the food; the sound is associated with failure and causes a withdrawal response. This will be irrelevant if the dog already has a mouthful of sandwich, because it has already succeeded and the techniques should not be used once the dog has possession.

For another example of how we can use conditioned avoidance learning let's return to the subject of dogs jumping up at visitors when they arrive at your house. In addition to them ignoring your dog until it sits quietly, you can ask them to fold their arms, break eye contact and freeze as soon as they hear you click the discs and throw them to the floor. After this has happened a few times they will not even be able to encourage your dog to jump up because your dog anticipates that if it does it will hear the sound of the discs and will fail to get any form of attention.

As we shall see, there is a range of situations in which this approach can be used to stop unwanted behaviour. It has been my experience that those dogs that have developed a sense of high status within their family/pack are less responsive to the use of the discs, and some dogs get annoyed at the frustration. Perhaps it is their general self-confidence that makes them less susceptible. Therefore it is often beneficial to address their mistaken sense of status first even if it seems unrelated to the problem (see Chapter 12)

NOTES

1. Pavlov, I.P. *Conditioned Reflexes* (Dover Publications 1924)

2. Thorndyke cited in: *Learning, Behaviour and Cognition* (2nd Ed) Lieberman, D.A. (Brooks/Cole Publishing Co. California 1983)

3. Skinner, B.F. Cited in: Psychology - *The Science of the Mind and Behaviour* (2nd Ed) Gross, R.D. (Hodder and Stoughton 1992)

4. Mugford R.A. *Canine Behavioural Therapy* Serpell J. (Ed) The Domestic Dog. Cambridge University Press

5. Fisher J. *Dogwise: The Natural Way to Train Your Dog* (Souvenir Press. London 1992)

6. Discussed in: Gray, J.A. *The Psychology of Fear and Stress* (Cambridge University Press 1987)

Further Reading

Gross R.D. *"Psychology - The Science of Mind and Behaviour"* (2nd Ed.) (Hodder and Stoughton 1992)

Lieberman, D.A. *Learning, Behaviour and Cognition* (2nd Ed.) (Brooks/Cole Publishing Co.California 1993)

Sautter, F.J., Glover, J.A. *Behaviour, Development and Training of the Dog* (Arco Publishing New York 1978)

— 6 —

Preventing and Curing Control Problems At Home

Although teaching our dogs to sit, heel, come, lie down and stay is beneficial, there is often a fundamental gap between what we expect from our dogs in training sessions and in everyday life. This does not

113

diminish the benefits of training, but we have to build on them by integrating training with other things we do with our dogs. This approach can help to prevent a range of behaviour problems. When these occur, it is often because we fail to communicate properly to the dog what we want it to do, and one of the ways we can help it is by guiding it and limiting its opportunity to do what we do not want it to do.

Look at the problem of getting Mrs Wellard's dog into the kitchen on page **83**. The problems she had had would not have occured if she taught her dog what she meant by the signal 'kitchen'. She could teach her dog to go into the kitchen when she gives the signal of the word 'kitchen' using the 'operant' training techniques described in chapter **5**. Although this is the most desirable form of training, the down side is that she would have to wait until her dog performed the action of its own accord, and it may take it a while to get the idea. She can help her dog to learn more quickly by guiding it.

The easiest method is to attach a thin piece of cord, about six feet in length, to a non-slip collar - one that buckles or fastens and won't tighten up, and let the dog drag it around the house. The cord has to be thin so it can slide under the end of open doors and around furniture. By picking up the line, Mrs Wellard can walk her dog to the kitchen, say the word 'kitchen' as it goes in and give it titbits which she produces from her pocket or from a dish in a convenient location in the kitchen itself. Mrs Wellard can then drop the line and let her dog follow her out of the kitchen if it wants to. Once her dog has developed an association between the word, going into the kitchen and the titbit, Mrs Wellard can start to dispense with the line, initially by leaving it on the ground so she can pick it up if she has to, and finally by removing it.

This 'house line' technique can also be used as a means of preventing a dog with a history of displaying growling or other defensive behaviours towards its owners from fearing it has entered into another confrontation, such as being told to move out of the way, to get off the furniture or out of its bed. By virtue of the fact that they don't have to touch their dog in situations like these, owners can reduce the likelihood that they may get bitten. This will be reduced still further when the dog starts to realise that it is rewarded when it responds to its owner's wishes. Whether you use it to help develop a response or to reduce the chance of conflict, the house line technique should be used whenever you have a spare moment and even when it is not necessary. Your dog eventually becomes so conditioned to respond that it will happily comply when it really matters.

A version of this technique can be used to train dogs that are not very good about entering the owner's house when called in from the garden. A dog failing to re-enter the house when called causes some owners a lot of difficulty, especially if it happens last thing at night or when they are trying to leave for work. The problem is particularly likely to occur if the dog has learnt that the longer it keeps it up the more attention it gets, but if it goes in the house, the owner goes away. or goes to bed. The garden line differs from the house line it that it can be about one and a half times as long and it is only put on before the dog goes into the garden. When it is time for the dog to come in, the owner can make their way to the line, pick it up and teach their dog to go into the house in the same way as dogs can be taught to go into the kitchen. This approach to curing the problem should be considered together with the recall techniques discussed in ch.apter **10**.

(It is possible that a dog will not want to go into the kitchen or enter the house because it is fearful of something in the kitchen or anxious about the owner's imminent departure. If you feel that one of these could apply to your dog see Chapter **13**)

Attention-seeking

Dogs can learn to perform various inappropriate or 'naughty' behaviours as attention seeking devices. To prevent this, you have to teach your dog to perform the right behaviour rather than simply trying to stop what it is doing. This is because the more you try to stop it, the more attention a dog gets and the more it will do it.

Sometimes people find it difficult to accept that their dog's problem behaviour is the result of attention-seeking because they give it attention all the time - but that's the point. Dogs can become attention junkies and learn to perform problem behaviour when the owners attention is temporarily withdrawn. Sometimes nuisance behaviours occur when the owner's telephone rings, the tune for a favourite programme starts, visitors arrive, etc. This is because these things allow the dog to predict that the owner's attention is going to be withdrawn.

Of course, the more the owners try and remonstrate with their dog, the more it will perform the behaviour. It does not matter to the dog whether these remonstrations involve being told off, provided that it gets the attention, but the owner's aggression can result in the dog learning to be defensive during attention-seeking scenarios.

Dogs can learn to perform some bizarre things as attention-seeking devices. These include stereotypic behaviours caused by the stress of anxiety or frustration. These behaviours are repeated over and over again, but they have no practical function other than that the performance of them reduces the dog's level of stress through its preoccupation, and through an alteration of brain chemistry which occurs while this is going on.

Such behaviours include tail chasing, catching imaginary flies, grooming or chewing itself until tissue damage is caused. Stereotypic

116

behaviours are, of course, serious behaviour problems in their own right that need specialist help, and you need to be aware that attempts to stop them, or laughing and looking at your dog when it performs them, often become a major reinforcement factor.

More usual attention-seeking devices include anything a dog learns is effective, such as restlessness when the family is trying to watch television, standing in front of the television, barking when its owner is using the phone, repeatedly asking to be let into the garden, or making passionate love to its bedding in front of visitors. I'm sure that readers can supply further exasperating examples!

Let's look at the common problem of the dog playing up when the family are watching television. If this happens in your household, changing the behaviour can be accomplished by totally ignoring your dog while you watch television - even by looking away from it and the screen until it lies down. Then, even if you have missed a vital bit of Star Trek, give your dog praise and a titbit. Keep rewarding it every so often to encourage your dog to stay in its resting position.

If, however, your dog's attention-seeking includes acts you cannot ignore because of the consequences, guiding it and limiting its options will help. Attach a house line to your dog's collar and sit down in a chair. Whilst holding the lead in your hand, pass it under your foot. The lead should be short enough to make your dog just a little uncomfortable if it is sitting up, but don't try and force it to lie down. Whatever your dog does now, ignore it until it chooses to lie down. When it does, say the word 'down' and give it a pat and a titbit. If your dog gets up again, ignore it immediately. Now through trial and error, your dog should learn that the way to keep getting attention is to stay down. The intervals between the periods of time you give your dog attention can be gradually increased. Practise the exercise at least once a day, the longer the session the better - no hardship when you are watching television. In a relatively short time, you will find your dog will learn to lie down without any need for the line.

After you have established the appropriate behaviour when you are on your own, you can use the same procedure when you have visitors if your dog tends to pester you while you are trying to chat. It's a good idea to ask friends to call round so you can use them as stooges in your training sessions. Your dog will gradually learn that if it lies down quietly when visitors are present, it will be handsomely rewarded.

Dogs that are difficult when visitors are present can reveal a more complex problem. For example, dogs that are over-dependent on their owners can become anxious, and dogs that have developed a sense of high status within the pack can become antagonistic whenever the owner's attention is withdrawn from them and, of course, visitors attract the owner's attention. The dog soon learns that jumping up at the visitor is an effective way of regaining the owner's attention.

Although the techniques described in this book as a means of stopping problem behaviours when visitors are present are wonderful in theory, the behaviour of the visitors themselves can often actively reinforce the dog's unwanted behaviour patterns. What is it that causes people deliberately to encourage a dog to give them a free wash and wipe despite the fact the owners are on the verge of bursting a blood vessel to get it back under control? Perhaps it's ego, politeness, empathy, or lack of understanding, but it is certainly not helpful. Under these circumstances it is best to remove your dog so that, in a calm and relaxed fashion, you can explain to the visitor what you are trying to achieve, and what it is you would like them to do to help you develop your dog's angelic behaviour! If you know that visitors are coming, it would be even better to brief them about how you would like them to behave towards the dog before they arrive.

Barking

Although barking is normal as a means of communication, in excess it is a cause of distress for the family, and especially for the neighbours. If the dog is generally responsive to its owners wishes, a quiet word is normally sufficient to stop the barking. Unfortunately where this does not work owners often attempt to silence their dog by shouting at it, but as the dog's communication skills don't extend to understanding English, it simply assumes the owners are barking too, and continues undeterred, or even redoubles its effort. Others discover barking makes their owner give them attention, if only to shout '*Shut up!*'

The fact that a dog barks for attention may not be readily apparent because it seems that it is barking for another reason, perhaps when it hears people passing the front of the owners' house which, being a territorial behaviour, is natural enough (See Chapter 14). However once a dog learns that its owners tell it to be quiet, its barking can become obsessive. This happens because the barking is rewarded twice, once by the fact that the people go away, and secondly because barking gets the owners attention. Eventually the dog can learn to exploit this to the point where it barks at almost nothing. Although a small amount of barking to alert people to the fact that someone has entered the vicinity of the owner's property is fine if there's an occasional intrusion up the garden path, barking at a succession of people passing the property can become an annoyance.

You can use many of the techniques described above as a means of modifying your dog's vocal attention-seeking behaviour: ignore what you don't want and reward what you do. For example, if every time your dog barks at you for attention you get up and walk out of the room, or silently turn your back, it will eventually learn that barking is counter-productive. When it chooses not to bark when it normally would have done, such as when someone walks past the house, give it a reward.

Believe it or not, one of the simplest ways to teach a dog to stop barking is to teach it to bark on your signal. First, find a way of enticing your dog to bark. You may find it will bark out of excitement if you hold its food bowl up in the air, or you may only need to use a titbit, or a toy. Tying your dog up safely will increase frustration, and the chance of it barking. When, with a bit of friendly teasing, your dog does bark, praise it and repeat the word 'speak!' each time it is apparent your dog is going to bark. If you do the exercise often enough, your dog will associate the word 'speak' with the act of barking and you will be able to get it to bark when you say speak. The point of the exercise is to then introduce the word, 'quiet!' or 'stop!' while your dog is barking, and give it a toy or titbit. If the exercise is repeated often enough, your dog will associate the signal to be quiet with the cessation of barking and a reward. (For non-stop barking when you are away, see Chapter 16)

Stealing and Guarding

Some dogs learn to get their owner's attention by stealing items that they are attracted to by the owner's scent, such as tea towels, underwear or used tissues. Although this may remain at a level of nuisance attention-seeking behaviour, it can develop into a serious problem. This is a common pattern:

1.   As a puppy, the dog learns that when it expresses the retrieve instinct by carrying a toy, the family are interested and give it attention. The novelty gradually wears off and they start to ignore the behaviour and continue to be preoccupied with domestic chores, watching television, talking to visitors etc. By chance, the

puppy finds that if it picks up an inappropriate item, such as a tissue out of someone's handbag and carries it, the family leap out of their chairs and attempt to regain possession of it. Therefore the puppy learns that picking up inappropriate items produces a response from the owners, and it is not ignored.

2.   After the initial amusement at its antics, the owners start to punish their growing dog when it has items they don't want it to have because taking them is 'naughty'. However this still provides the juvenile with the reward of attention, so the behaviour continues to be reinforced. In response to its owner's aggressive behaviour, it learns that once it has stolen an item, it has to be prepared to defend itself and will often run under a table or somewhere else where it can do this more easily. When it growls defensively at its owners because it anticipates their aggression, they punish it - which makes it more likely that it will be defensive next time. If it is also confident in its status as a high-ranking member of the pack, it may also be inclined to guard its trophy for its own sake. Those with less confidence sometimes try and swallow the item quickly to stop the owners from getting it. Getting back items the dog has swallowed - such as a pair of tights - via surgery, can be an expensive business.

3.   Repeated conflict scenarios over items the dog has taken possession of can eventually result in its preparedness to display defensive behaviour in other situations where it feels it may be confronted, such as when asked to move out of the way, or when someone approaches it when it is on its bed or wherever it goes to when it has got a trophy.

To prevent this process developing in your own home, all you have to do is make sure that you do not ignore appropriate behaviour just because it is convenient. So every so often you should give your dog attention whilst it is lying down quietly, chewing its chew etc, and reward your dog when it brings things to you (Also see Chapter 7).

121

One of the ways you can overcome the problem of stealing and guarding and other attention-seeking behaviours is by adopting a policy of only interacting with your dog when you initiate it. You can also consider this option if you feel that your dog is becoming overly-dependent upon your attention. Over a period of time your dog's expectations will be altered, which will reduce the likelihood of problem behaviours being displayed as attention-seeking devices, and of it being distressed when you are preoccupied. However this approach does not mean that your dog will go without attention. You can fuss it as much as you like, just as long as *you* initiate the attention.

A variant on this theme is to teach your dog that there are periods of time when it cannot expect to receive attention. Many dogs learn this themselves by picking up on stimuli that allow them to discriminate. For example, many dogs learn that when the television goes on or their owner starts the housework they can not expect to get attention, and will lie down or take themselves off to bed. They will have learnt this through experience, but not all dogs have such consistent learning opportunities.

For those dogs prone to severe attention-seeking problems, we can provide a stimulus that allows them to anticipate what to expect consistently. This is important, because an unpredictable environment can induce stress. To achieve this, put a novel item in an obvious location. The item can be as simple as a towel hung over the living-room door. Then ignore whatever your dog does. When the period of 'no attention' is to end, the item should be put in another location or out of sight. Over a period of time, your dog should learn that from the presence of the item in the 'no attention' position it can predict that it cannot get an response from you. Once an association between the item and your dog's expectation of not receiving attention has been developed, it should be possible to put the novel item in the 'no attention' location when you are preoccupied when watching television, talking to visitors, talking on the telephone etc., and your dog will remain relaxed throughout.

APBC member John Fisher used to tell a story that shows how effective this technique can be. Clients of his had been advised to ignore their dog for periods of time each day as part of a programme for modifying its behaviour. But however much they tried, their attempts were unwittingly sabotaged by family members entering the house throughout the day at different times, and greeting the dog because they were unaware that a period of ignoring the dog was supposed to be in operation. So they decided to put a particular ornament on the coffee table whenever the dog was to be ignored. It did not take long for the dog to learn the significance of the ornament when it appeared on the table - and it went to bed!

The Interactive Key

If a very serious attention-seeking problem has already developed, it can be advantageous to give your dog a way it can get attention by re-directing it onto a toy. The toy should be like no other toy in the house, although you can have several of the same throughout the house, and in the garden. Ideally it should be a toy, or item, of convenient size that your dog likes to carry. It should be large enough for you to see when it is in your dog's mouth, and to prevent it swallowing it, but small enough to avoid your dog crashing it into the furniture and the back of your legs.

Once you have selected your item, you can continue to fuss over your dog when you initiate it, but ignore all of your dog's attention-seeking behaviours. When your dog happens to pick up the toy, give your dog lots of attention, but if it drops it, switch off again and ignore it. Over a period of time your dog will learn that holding the toy is the method by which it can solicit a response, and will subsequently use it to say 'I need a hug please'. It is important that you do not ignore your dog when it is holding the toy in its mouth so that it can predict that it will get a response. The **interactive key,** as I like to call it, should never be used as a play item or removed from your dog's mouth so as to prevent it from becoming associated with competition (see Chapter **12**) or confrontation.

You may think that your dog will be forever thrusting the interactive key at you to get attention. In fact you should find that once your dog has learnt that carrying the key means it will never be ignored, it will become more relaxed about getting attention and need less of it. This is because it can predict a response which contrasts with the intermittent responses and their unpredictable style it was getting when it displayed nuisance attention-seeking behaviours. We have already seen that intermittent responses would have had a strong reinforcing effect on the behaviour you did not want and their unpredictable nature would have caused stress.

To help ensure the successful implementation of the interactive key technique, make sure that your dog does not have the opportunity to gain access to inappropriate attention-seeking articles. This can be made easier by not allowing your dog into bedrooms.

If you have a real problem with particular items that are repeatedly stolen, you can use entrapment by placing a spring-loaded cap firing trap (see page **105**) under the item so that when your dog moves the potential trophy there is a small 'explosion'. If you make sure that the only items that are available to steal are set-ups, your dog should learn to avoid them in future, unless it learns to anticipate when it will go bang because it can smell the cap. To prevent this happening put a dab of cheap aftershave or perfume you would not dream of wearing on each of the items you use for entrapment, e.g. shoes. Once your dog has learnt to avoid the traps, make sure that all the shoes in the house are occasionally dabbed with the scent. You can gradually return to a more relaxed attitude about the items you leave lying about once you have successfully modified your dog's behaviour.

Digging

Some owners are troubled by their dog digging in their garden or digging up their lawns. This can be a manifestation of the instinct to dig out a shallow pit to lie in or to bury food, such as bones. Sometimes dogs may continue to dig once they have started because they get some enjoyment from it. As with other aspects of a dog's behaviour, digging can become a learned attention-seeking device: it is a good way of getting the owners to bang on the windows or come outside to tell it to stop!

One way of stopping your dog digging in a particular area (such as a precious flower bed), is to set up a garden hose and sprinkler. The sprinkler should be placed in this location and hose should be attached to a tap inside the house. When your dog starts to dig you can make it rain by turning the tap on. Even those dogs that like playing with water when their owners use the hose are often perturbed when this happens without warning. If this is the case with your dog, turn the tap off again as soon as it gets off that part of your garden.

The best way of getting your dog to avoid digging where you do not want it to is to give it a place where it *can* dig: the canine equivalent of a sand pit. To do this, dig out an area of garden to a depth of about one or two feet and fill it with sand, loose soil or soil mixed with sand. Mark the boundary of this area, with logs for example. If you bury toys and any bones or chews you buy your dog in this pit, your dog can have great fun digging them up again. This should satisfy its need for digging. However, don't give your dog a place to dig if it doesn't have a digging problem. You may otherwise develop a behaviour you don't want.

——— 7. ———

Teaching Your Dog To Bring
Things To You

Of all the exercises you can teach your dog, the retrieve must be one
of the most rewarding. It is also useful in the prevention of behaviour
problems because you can teach your dog or puppy to bring you
anything it has picked up, instead of running off with it and leading
you a merry dance. Once your dog has learnt that it can bring things

to you and be confident that you will be pleased rather than cross, the likelihood of it learning to take things and guard them will be reduced. Playing 'fetch' can be a useful way of exercising your dog. However, if your pet is obsessed with chasing, this game will make things worse. Once you have successfully established the retrieve, switch to search games instead (see p. 158)

To get your dog to retrieve reliably you have to get the basics right. The best time to start is during puppyhood. If your puppy gets into the habit of picking up anything and everything you could be making a rod for your own back, because it will start to do it all the time. To reduce the risk of this occuring, make sure you provide it with the things you want to teach it to bring to you, and keep other things out of reach as much as possible. Whether you are starting your training with a puppy or an older dog, the procedure is the same. As with all teaching sessions, keep these exercises short and sweet, so that your dog doesn't get bored and stays keen to play the next time. Little and often is the key.

Getting Started

The best way to get results from training sessions is to teach an exercise sequence backwards. Let me explain.

A dog can learn to perform several different 'behaviours' in a sequence to get to the final reward. To achieve this, the different elements are taught separately, and backwards. **Retrieve** is a good example of this. The exercise consists of the following elements:

- The dog runs from your side
- Picks something up
- Brings it to you
- Gives it to you.

127

If you teach each stage separately, your dog will know what is expected of it when the elements of the sequence are linked together. So you should teach 'give' first, then 'bring', then 'pick it up', then 'fetch it.' (You can try this on yourself: select a short poem and learn the last line first. Then learn the second from last line, and so on, back to the beginning. You will eventually know the whole poem and never get flustered, because you will always know what comes next!)

The first step is to teach your dog to give you something. This may sound straightforward, but it is in fact the part of the process that many training enthusiasts sometimes have trouble with. Normally problems are encountered because the dog has been unwittingly taught to do the 'wrong' thing. The most common mistake during training is commanding the dog to "give" an item when it is still holding onto it.

You can imagine the scene: the dog gets to the handler with an item held in its mouth. When it hears the words 'Good boy' it seems that it is being praised for holding on and, so it keeps doing it. Then it hears the words "Give", "Leave", "Thank You" or whatever the owner tends to use. This is said when the dog is still holding onto the item so it seems to the dog that the word means "hang on", so that is what it does. After a few sessions of this, the owner can start hissing "Give" through gritted teeth, while the dog hangs on for dear life, because that is what it has been trained to do.

The owner will then use the stock answer of grabbing the top of the dog's muzzle and pushing his or her fingers against its mouth. This forces the skin against the dog's teeth and the discomfort causes it to open its mouth and let go of the item. This has not made the dog learn to bring things back, and also has taught it to stay out of reach. But by using the positive techniques described below, these problems can be avoided.

Stage 1

Sit in a chair and hold a toy in such a position as will encourage your dog or puppy to take it from you. (You may have to stimulate its interest by playing with the toy.) When your dog has taken the toy, say "Hold". Move your hands away, and gently say "Hold" in an encouraging voice whilst your dog is holding the item. Before your dog gets tired of holding on, put your hand to the item and wait until it lets go.

As it does, say 'give' or whatever word you want your dog to associate with giving you things, and give it lots of praise and a titbit to reinforce the response. After you have practised this often enough, your dog will learn to associate 'give' (or your chosen word) with letting go of an object. You will be able to use the word whenever you want it to release something.

Stage 2

Put some toys or other items in a group on the floor. Whenever your dog happens to pick up an item, drop onto your haunches and encourage it to come to you. If your dog has a particular place it likes to go to, move to that location first so that it is more inclined to come to you. If your dog drops the item, stand up and ignore it until it picks it up again, then encourage it to come to you.

When your dog gets to you, put your hand to the item and wait until it lets go. As it does, say the word you want your dog to associate with giving you things and give it lots of praise, titbits etc. to reinforce the response.

Stage 3

You will notice that so far we have looked at the last part of the retrieve, the bringing of the item to you. Once you have done this you can teach your dog the first part - going to get it. Make sure the item you want your dog to retrieve is obvious, because it happens to be the only item present. The item should be of a convenient size and safe for your dog to carry.

Whilst your dog is kept sitting by your side - either by holding its collar or using the signal for it to stay where it is, if you have progressed that far (see page134) - throw the item away from you. When the item has stopped moving you may encourage your dog to go to it. As your dog runs to the item, say encouragingly, *fetch it!* or *get it!* or whatever other words you want your dog to associate with finding things. This word will eventually become so linked to search behaviour that you will be able to trigger a search immediately.

I like to say *"where is it"* in an excited voice and slur the words together. I find it difficult to sound authoritarian using this phrase, and it is important that the dog is not pressurised into fetching something, but does so because it is enjoying it and learns from success. When your dog picks up the item, encourage it to come to you as described above, which it will know how to do because it has already learnt it.

—— 8. ——

Teaching Your Dog To Leave and to Stay

Teaching your dog to leave

Many dogs learn to stop showing interest in something or chasing when told to do so, without too many problems. But just as many leave their owners frustrated, as they call their dogs until they are blue in the face and are eventually forced to get hold of their dog to drag it away from the object of interest.

How well a dog will respond to its owner varies from situation to situation. For example, if someone walks past you both, your dog is less likely to be stimulated into giving chase than if the person is running. The problem can be made worse if a dog perceives its owner's attempts to stop it as encouragement, or that the pair of them are baying after the same quarry!

131

The way your dog is likely to respond depends on its innate drives and the type of dog it is. For example, Labradors are a breed renowned for their interest in food, and so may be harder to call away from food than a Sheltie. But if a Labrador prefers the smell of meat to cake, it may be harder to call it away from a rancid bone it has found in a field than a whole cake shop.

You can increase the chances of your dog responding when you call it away from something by putting the emphasis on what you want it to do, rather than what you do not want it to do. Start the process by teaching your dog or puppy the word 'off' in the same way as it can be taught to stop playbiting or mouthing (see page 54) using titbits or a toy.

Once you have established a response to the 'off' technique, you can adapt it to teach your dog to leave things and come to you. The first stage of this adaptation requires that you go through the 'off' sequence, but wait until your dog looks you in the face. As soon as it does, give it lots of praise and back off a few paces whilst continuing to praise it. When it catches up with you give it the titbit or toy you are using as a reinforcer, as well as continued praise. Repeat the process several times in the first session, and then again over several sessions, to develop your dog's response to the point where it has learnt that when it hears you say 'off' it looks straight at you and moves towards you.

The next stage involves rolling a toy for your dog to encourage it to show interest in chasing it. Start by rolling the toy very slowly, but if even rolling it slowly produces too much stimulation because your dog is obsessed with toys or movement, place the toy on the floor instead. When your dog moves towards the toy say the word 'off', and as it turns to look at you, back off while encouraging it to follow you. When it catches up give it lots of praise and a titbit or another toy from your pocket, whichever it likes most. The more promise your dog shows, the more you can make the toy move before calling your dog away from it. With practice you will soon be able to call your dog away from the toy, however stimulating it is, and mix 'off' training with retrieving games.

You can take things further by asking family and friends to become diversions for you to call your dog away from. Start this conditioning in your home and garden before progressing to other areas where there is likely to be more distraction. The people trying to distract your dog have one simple rule: they must not say its name. They can however run about, play with a toy and generally behave in a manner your dog will find exciting and attractive. In the same way that you gradually increased your dog's interest in the toy, your helper can build up the amount of distraction your dog is presented with. The rate of increase should, as always, be in keeping with your dog's progress. Get your dog to leave them by saying '*off*' as before and encourage it to return to you. If your dog continues to be interested in the helpers, ask them to stand still and avoid any interaction or eye contact with your dog. In this way your dog will learn that if it continues to pursue something when you say '*off*', the distraction suddenly becomes boring and coming to you is a more interesting proposition.

When you think your dog is ready, use the technique to call your dog away from all sorts of things, such as cakes on the coffee table, in addition to those it may want to chase or investigate. For example, you can use it to teach your dog to come away from other dogs. The technique is particularly useful for treating dogs that show aggression towards other dogs caused by frustrative play (see p.189) because they are given something to do which removes the frustration. If you have a dog that is aggressive towards other dogs or people when it is on the lead, you can use the technique to get it to concentrate on you and to ignore other dogs or people when you pass them. Although your dog will not be able to run to you when it is on the lead it will be able to look at you rather than the other dog or person when it hears the magic word!

Teaching your dog to stay

The traditional way of teaching a dog to remain where it is involves saying the word '*stay*' in a "don't move or else" tone of voice that is intended to nail it to the ground. Some dogs find this process so intimidating that they move towards their owners in a submissive manner. You can understand why. From the dog's point of view, its owner is walking away and giving an aggressive signal. Obviously the only thing to do is stop doing whatever it is that is making them aggressive and show submissive behaviour.

To compound the misunderstanding, the owner now sees his dog's act of creeping towards him as disobedience, and reprimands it before putting it back into position and then repeats the process over again. Eventually, most dogs learn that the only way to avoid a telling off is to stay where they are. You can often identify these by the fact that they look cowed when their owner returns to them.

It is much kinder to teach your dog to stay where it is by helping it understand what you want it to do. As we have seen this means that reinforcement must come at the right time. Once your dog is lying down at your signal, you can build this up into a stay by taking a step away from it then stepping forward again and praising it for staying down. While you are moving, hold your hand out in front of you, with your palm facing towards your dog. This will eventually become a signal your dog will recognise as 'do nothing'. Each time you return to praise your dog, crouch down so as to avoid encouraging it to sit up. In each session repeat this process several times in succession before giving another signal to tell your dog the exercise is over.

After several sessions you will find it easy to build up the number of paces you take away from your dog before returning to it to praise it for lying down. You can then pause when you are a few paces away, and thereby build up the amount of time it will stay lying down.

Although 'stay' is what we want our dogs to do, we do not have to use the word 'stay' as the signal. You can use reinforcement of the behaviour it is doing instead. For example, if your dog is lying down, you can keep returning to your dog and praising it by saying 'down' in a gentle voice. You will know if you are doing it right because your dog will look relaxed and be content to do nothing until you are ready to move on to something else.

When you want to release your dog from a 'stay', give it a clear signal that the exercise is over, such as walking around it once, then saying 'finish'. You could also give it something else to do, such as walking by your side.

— 9. —

Training Classes

Attending dog training classes is a way of developing your handling skills under the guidance of a good trainer. Beginners' courses last a few weeks and concern themselves with teaching the basics. Most progressive clubs also run puppy socialisation classes. In these classes, puppies are given the opportunity to socialise with others in their age group, so that they can get used to other dogs and their owners.

Even dogs belonging to experienced handlers benefit from attending classes, because they can learn to be responsive to their owner's wishes despite the presence of distractions. If you catch the training bug, there will also be the opportunity to go on to train to competition standard. You might also like to try competing in working trials or joining in the exciting sports of agility or flyball.

You should not, however, view a dog training club as a place to take your dog to overcome its behaviour problems such as fear or aggression - particularly not aggression towards other dogs. All too often, owners find that their dog is aggressive to other dogs and decide that they will take it to dog training classes so it can meet others, without realising what impact this will have on the dogs that are there. If your dog is aggressive to other dogs, attending classes should not be considered until the latter stages of curing the problem.

Choosing The Right Teacher

Finding the right training environment can be difficult, but if you know what you are looking for you should be able to avoid the pitfalls. Organised training falls into three main categories: dog training clubs, professional tuition and residential training. This last type is inappropriate for most family pets, and is usually used by very experienced handlers who have no time to train their own dogs.

What to Watch Out For

Normally it is as important for the owner to be educated as it is for the dog, but sadly, there are some establishments only too happy to relieve the unwary of their money. On one occasion it was reported that a training kennels returned a West Highland Terrier to its elderly owners after it had been "trained". The couple were given a video of what the dog could do for the trainer. Within a few days, any improvement the dog showed when it first returned home wore off because the owners hadn't a clue how to achieve or reinforce the things their dog had learnt.

Happily, most owners go to their local dog training club or to a professional trainer who can provide a competent service. Training clubs normally have a nominal charge to cover the cost of hiring the hall, and are usually organised by enthusiasts. However this apparent idyll can sometimes create problems. For example, when a club is having difficulty finding enough instructors, the blind may end up leading the blind because there is a temptation for the organisers to ask relatively inexperienced members to teach, simply because they have done well with their own dogs.

Choosing Your Training Club

If you have a choice of various clubs or professional trainers, arrange to go along to observe before you start taking your dog. The most important factor for you to consider is the method of training employed. If it seems to be harsh and punitive, with lots of shouting and a tendency for dogs to be jerked about on check chains while being marched up and down in a regimented fashion, this is not the club for you.

It should be very obvious whether the trainers you observe teach positive ways of training, not least because their methods get the best results from dogs of all types without inducing stress. But believe it or not, this is not always a popular approach with some owners, who prefer the bullying trainer down the road because this is what they think dog training is all about.

Does The Trainer Care?

It should be obvious to you that the trainers are interested in your aspirations, and accept that you may not want to achieve the doggy equivalent of dressage. They should also display a flexibility of approach to you, the other owners and your various pets of different types and temperaments.

Sadly, some trainers try to lump everyone together, heedless of the number of owners who stop attending because they have been demotivated or frustrated at their dogs lack of success when compared with the star pupils such as Border Collies.

Most of the people who run dog training classes don't get paid and have not gained any formal qualifications in the subject. They teach because they enjoy dog training, but there is no standardisation for them to conform to. You may be interested to know that the Association of Pet Dog Trainers was established in the UK in 1995, in an attempt to make it possible for dog owners to be directed to someone who has been accredited as a user of kind, effective methods of training. Details on contacting the APDT are at the end of the book.

The Right Class

In general, look for classes that are not too large. There is little benefit in walking round and round a village hall, shoe-horned into a group of dogs that are nose to tail. An optimum number in a class is eight. This allows the person taking the class enough time for observation, and the opportunity to give proper coaching. If an assistant is present the class can be larger, but low numbers in a small space also help to reduce the chance that a dog may try to lunge at others in the group. This is important, because you don't want to go to dog training classes only to find that your dog learns to be defensive in the presence of other dogs because it has been attacked.

If you want to take a puppy to socialisation classes, the important aspects to look for are:

1. The exclusion of older dogs.

2. An upper joining limit of eighteen weeks of age.

3. Socialisation opportunities, where the puppies mix with each other and the other owners present, need to be combined with some teaching to help the puppies respond to their owners' wishes. It is important that puppies don't learn to run amok and ignore their owners whenever they are in the presence of other dogs.

Practice makes perfect

A large number of owners go to dog training classes and are disappointed with the results. Normally the blame for this cannot be laid at the feet of the people giving the lessons. Many an instructor sighs in despair as, at the end of a perfect half-hour of walking neatly to heel, the dogs then madly mob out of the door together, dragging their owners behind them as if they were in a chariot race.

It is easy to understand why dogs are well-behaved in the training class and not so well behaved elsewhere - when you look at it from the dog's point of view. Often the class is the only place in which the owners give their dogs undivided attention, and if the dogs do not execute the task requested they will encourage it to comply, whereas they may be less diligent at home.

The instructor's most commonly used phrase is something along the lines of: 'You come here to learn how to train your dogs at home, not to teach them to be better behaved for the rest of the week'. Failure will be more likely if the only place a dog associates with training is the village hall. To develop what they have learnt in class, a dog and its owner have to practice, over and over again: first of all in ideal conditions where there are few distractions. Gradual progress can then be made to noisier or more exciting places.

— 10. —

Preventing and Curing Control Problems Away From Home

Pulling on a Lead

You don't have to be very observant to realise that the most common problem owners experience outside the home is their dog's tendency to pull on the lead. Even many of the dogs that learn not to pull at a training class tend to drag their owners from pillar to post once they escape the confines of the village hall.

If you experience this problem, the first thing to consider is why your dog pulls. Although all dogs that pull do so because of a lack of appropriate training, their motivations for pulling are various: getting to a favourite destination, like the park; going to the furthest extent of the lead to sniff every scent mark left behind by other dogs, or even because of the dog's misplaced sense of high status within the family (see chapter 12) allow it to decide the pace and direction of the walk.

141

Reasons For Pulling

Pulling on the lead has a lot to do with incentive. The more reason a dog has to pull, the more it will do so. Reducing the incentive will discourage it. For example, if your dog is inclined to pull because it associates going for a walk with going to the park - you can tell this because it will not pull on the way home - you can adopt different strategies.

Take it for walks that avoid the park, or repeatedly walk towards the park, but then either walk past or simply turn and walk away when you get there. Both should work eventually, but you would deprive your dog of its free exercise, so you will have to compensate by walking further yourself.

Pain avoidance is another common cause of pulling - specifically the pain inflicted on the dog's neck from a check chain. This sort of collar forms a noose shape before being put over the dog's head. It can be pulled tight and, if fitted properly, it will loosen up once the lead becomes slack.

The check chain is commonly (but mistakenly) called a choke chain, and consequently many owners misunderstand its intended function. They think that when the dog pulls, the chain tightens and chokes the dog - discouraging it from pulling. This is not the case - in reality the dog often continues to pull, but gasps a lot. Although I would not recommend the use of a check chain in most circumstances, this is the prescribed way to use it:

1.   When the dog walks too far in front, the handler's arm is thrown forward to make the lead and chain go slack.

2.   Then, with a quick movement, the lead is jerked back across the handler's body so the chain closes quickly and inflicts pain - which, for the dog, must be like being bitten on the neck.

Trainers recommending this technique normally instruct the handler to shout '*heel!*' in the belief the dog will know what it is being corrected for - and that it will eventually work out what it is supposed to do. In other words, this method of training requires that the dog keeps on finding out what it must not do in order to avoid getting jerked on the neck. This method can induce stress which is not conducive to training, and if the method backfires some dogs learn that being on the lead with the owner is an unpleasant experience, increasing the tendency to pull to get away.

Another point to consider here is the fact that if the word '*heel*' is said when the dog is ahead of the handler it will become associated with the act of walking ahead. So if it could speak, the dog's response to the handler saying '*heel!*' might be 'yes, that's right, walking three feet ahead as requested......urkk!!...what did you do that for?' In turn, the owner may become frustrated because the dog has not learnt to walk by their side when they give this command and in consequence their techniques may get harsher, and the dog increasingly unresponsive.

The check chain can be an effective piece of equipment in experienced hands, but it is by no means the best, nor the most humane technique, particularly because of its potential to cause physical injury to the neck. One of the reasons why check chains have persisted is because some trainers believe they work well in their classes and that all owners are capable of using them. They then blame the owners for not using theirs properly away from class when they find their dog pulls.

Dogs are inclined to walk at their owner's side at a training class, however, because all they have to look forward to is going round the village hall again. If a dog walks ahead of its owner or pulls to one side in a training school that uses check chains and punitive methods, it is jerked on the neck. This is an experience it learns to avoid by staying close to the handler. But when out and about the dog is likely to have greater motivation to pull, because it anticipates a pleasant destination or wants to investigate the things it passes.

The owner may then use the chain with the prescribed technique, or incorrectly, but either way the dog keeps walking. So although the dog has the experience of the jerk, it keeps moving in a direction it wants to go. Significantly, animals will learn to tolerate an unpleasant experience if it comes before something rewarding. Applying something unpleasant like a jerk on the neck with a check chain is unnecessary because the withdrawal of something the dog wants is punishment enough.

It is more important to change the whole emphasis of the exercise. Rather than teaching your dog not to pull, concentrate on what you really want to achieve by rewarding it for walking quietly by your side. As always, short (a few minutes at most) training sessions are most effective.

The best way to teach heel work is to teach a dog or puppy to walk by your side off the lead, in your garden, using a toy or a piece of food as a lure.

When your dog is walking next to you, say 'heel' every so often, and reward your dog. In this way, the word will become associated with what you want. Once your dog stays by your side so that it can receive the reward, you can progress to dispensing with the lure and producing the toy or food from your pocket instead. At this point you can progress to using a lead and then practising away from home.

When walks begin away from home, there will naturally be more excitement, and more tendency to pull. If your dog wants to sniff

Walking to heel using a lure

something, you can use the 'off' technique (see Chapter 8). If it is beginning to drag you along in its eagerness to get somewhere or something, try the following exercises to teach the dog to associate pulling with an unrewarding effect. For your dog, there's nothing more disappointing than achieving the opposite to what was intended!

145

How To Stop Pulling

Start your walk as normal, with your dog on a fairly long lead attached to a collar that will not slip over its head. If the location you are using is free of traffic and other hazards, you can use an extending lead. When your dog starts to pull, allow it to go ahead. Then as it does, start to walk backwards - by this, I literally mean reverse, don't turn around. Don't be tempted to speak.

The tightening of the lead should surprise your dog, and when it looks round to see what has happened, it will see you walking away. This and the fact that the lead is guiding it in that direction, should encourage your dog to come trotting back to you. As it does, give it lots of praise and encouragement. The nearer your dog gets, the more enthusiastic your voice should become, but keep on walking backwards (at least six big paces) until it has caught up.

Once you are together again, set off in the original direction of your walk. Very soon your dog will start to pull ahead again. When it does, repeat the process. After a few repetitions, you may find your dog comes back to you willingly enough but sets off again too quickly - in which case walk backwards another six paces straight away.

On your initial sessions you may find yourself walking backwards more than forwards! But after a while your dog should be walking by your side, glancing up every so often to see whether you are about to walk backwards again. When it is walking well and particularly when it looks back at you, praise your dog and say '*heel*'. This associates the word with what you want it to do, thereby making walking by your side a rewarding experience it will be keen to repeat. As an extra incentive, you can intermittently give titbits by producing them from your pocket. Hopefully, if you apply the technique consistently, your dog will quickly learn to walk quietly by your side, despite any amount of temptation to walk ahead.

A typical head collar

Walks for pleasure and for exercise can be combined with walks conducted specifically for the purpose of teaching your dog to walk well. In next to no time, it should be possible to walk your dog in an orderly fashion and combine the expedition with some free exercise every time.

Punctuate your walk to and from the free running area with a lot of *'Sit's!'* This will help develop general control - at every road crossing for example. It can also be advantageous to conduct a short session of training exercises just before you let your dog off the lead to have a run. This will reduce its enthusiasm for pulling to get to where it has a run, and help to associate the free running environment with a level of control.

Harnesses and Head collars

If all else fails and you still find yourself being dragged along while your shoe leather burns away, you may find a head-collar such as a Halti or Gentle Leader useful. In some cases people find that the use of an anti-pulling harness is effective. Head-collars and anti-pulling harnesses have the effect of offsetting the power-weight ratio in the owner's favour, making it difficult for the dog to pull them along. You can combine the use of a head collar or harness with the technique described above to teach your dog that pulling is counter productive - but be sure to attach your lead to both the head-collar and an ordinary collar, just in case the head-collar comes off when you are walking backwards.

Recall

Picture this familiar scene: The sound of 'Rover......Rover! come here boy,' drifts across the town park to the unconcerned dog that's busily investigating a clump of long wet grass. He looks up lethargically and spots his frustrated owner calling. It is a cold,

148

damp evening and the owner wants to get home. Safe in the knowledge that his owner is where he left him, Rover continues to investigate the grass. This scenario is played out every day, with Rover deciding to return only when he is good and ready.

Some owners take their dogs for granted, and eventually show little or no appreciation for the fact that their dog comes back when called. This contrasts dramatically with their behaviour when they first let the dog off the lead in a public place. Then the owner's voice will have a sense of encouragement in its tone that betrays his or her apprehension about whether it would come back, or run off despite the training carried out at home and on the lead. When the dog does come back to its owner, it is smothered by the relief-driven praise it received, making it willing to come back with more enthusiasm on the next occasion.

As the days pass and the dog's recall becomes reliable, the owner may start to take it for granted, and gone are the euphoric displays when the dog returns. As a result, the dog may start to amble up in its own time, or allow itself to be distracted with increasing regularity. The owner may feel frustrated that their dog does not come back as quickly as it used to, but why should it? What is the incentive? Having the lead clipped on because the owner wants to go home? I don't think so.

There are many ways we can improve our dog's recall, or, better still, prevent poor recall from developing in the first place. A most important consideration is our ability to communicate: without it, the dog simply fails to realise that it is being called.

If we use our dog's name when we want it to come to us, an association will develop; but if it frequently hears its name when it is not required to respond - or, worse still, when it is being reprimanded - it is quite possible that, eventually, it won't respond

149

well to its name, or will be reluctant to return. To avoid any confusion it is vital that we only use our dog's name when we want it to come to us, so that the name becomes an unambiguous signal.

If your dog has already tired of responding to its name, or has developed a negative association with it, or you just want to use its name as you chat away to it, you could try introducing a new recall signal. How about a whistle? There's no need for anything fancy like a special dog whistle that no-one can hear. A normal, plastic, pea-less whistle will do. An advantage of using the whistle is that it is the same sound whoever uses it, making it easier for all the family to achieve the same results. Before the whistle technique will work for you, however, your dog will have to develop an association between the sound and the behaviour you want. If you can start teaching this to a puppy, so much the better.

Whether you are using a whistle or your voice, the first step is to teach the recall in your house and garden, if possible. Get someone to hold your dog's collar while you walk away with its dinner. Place the bowl on the floor and blow the whistle to call your dog to the food. The other person should let go of your dog's collar so that it can run towards you.

By dividing your dog's food into portions, you can repeat this process several times in each session. After a few days you can use the same technique with titbits or a favourite toy, initially as described above, and then less formally by carrying some titbits in your pocket. When your dog is least expecting it, blow the whistle or call it and when your dog comes to you give it a titbit and lots of praise.

Once you are sure the association between the whistle and running to you for food has been developed, you can start to apply the techniques on walks. Remember that you will need to change the frequency of the rewards to get the best results. (see p. 101)

Extra Control

If you feel that you need to maintain a higher level of control, or test the reliability of your dog before you let it off the lead, (something you may be particularly inclined to do if you have given a home to an older dog), you can use an extending lead to give it more freedom. If your dog continues to respond well to your signal to come back, you can progress to attaching a long line of around 10 metres (approximately 30 feet), to your dog's securely buckled collar in those locations where you will eventually want to let it off the lead. A smaller dog does not need such a long line.

The trailing line will provide you with the opportunity to tread on it to prevent your dog from escaping, without having to chase after it. Obviously this technique requires a degree of concentration, but the length of the line will give you a good margin of error. If you suspect or are convinced that you dog will run off, you can hold the opposite end of the line, but let the rest drag on the ground so as to avoid it getting tangled in knots.

If your dog's keenness to run off and ignore you is particularly strong, the long line can be combined with the use of the aversion technique of the rattle can or conditioned avoidance using training disks behind it, (see page 105) so as to interrupt any interest in distractions. To do this successfully, throw the device making the rattle to the floor whenever your dog is distracted. Whenever aversion or avoidance techniques are used, ensure that you appear uninvolved with the rattling sounds.

When your dog looks around, drop down into an inviting body posture, and combine this with some soothing words. This will encourage your dog to come to you for rewards and praise. Set off again, but watch your dog carefully. As soon as you think that it has

151

stopped concentrating on you and has become preoccupied with something else, repeat the process.

After a few repetitions of this you should find that your dog will stay close to you because it is beginning to feel insecure. This is useful because it will mean that your dog will be as unsure about leaving your side as it was when it was a puppy, providing a great opportunity for developing the behaviour you want from scratch.

After employing the long line technique over a period of time, with or without the rattle-can or training disks, with luck you will feel that it is redundant. However, to remove the line at this stage may cause your dog to revert to the pattern of behaviour it displayed before you started, because the presence of the line is associated with the new learning. To prevent this, gradually reduce the weight of the line by cutting off 30cm sections over a period of time, depending on the progress your dog makes. The dog's association of the line with the training and its inhibitory effect will be gradually withdrawn as it gets lighter. If you feel that your dog's behaviour is reverting because you have tried to make progress too quickly, return to an earlier stage by using a longer line.

Recalling Your Dog

We must not forget forms of language other than sound when recalling our dogs. Remember that the most inviting body posture is to get down on your haunches with your arms and knees wide open. Also, remember facial expressions - even if it is raining and you're cold and fed up, Fido must believe you are delighted he has come back!

I'm sure that anyone reading this book will realise by now that it is wrong to tell your dog off for not coming back sooner when it eventually gets to you. This is because it can only associate the telling off with the act of coming back, and will be hesitant or even avoid you next time you call it. Rather than not return at all, many dogs will stay just out of arm's reach to avoid any unpleasantness.

There are some other less obvious turn-offs. A common one is only calling the dog when it's time to go home. This is because the recall and lead attachment become associated with the end of the walk, and so the dog has no incentive to return. You can avoid this by repeatedly calling your dog throughout the walk, putting it on the lead and giving a titbit before letting it go and play again.

Another big turn-off can be formal obedience. Returning to the owner can become more of a chore than a pleasure for a dog if it is compelled to sit straight in front or come round to heel, every time it is called. Make sure that your dog gets lots of fuss and attention when it gets back with no formality when you are out for a walk. If you really must practise formal recall training, try doing it intermittently during your walk so that formalities and fun are mixed together. Conversely, if your dog's recall is over-enthusiastic - to the point where it is in danger of knocking you over or breaking your legs, teaching it to sit straight in front of you when it returns could be just the thing you need to cool it off a little.

Bores Are Ignored

Guard against predictability (Boring Handler Syndrome). Changing direction on the walk will stop your dog from taking you for granted. When you call your dog, don't stand still - run off, or run backwards to encourage a quick recall. Whenever possible, hide in positions from which you can observe your dog to provoke it into being concerned about where you are and to come running to find you. In turn this should make it more inclined to stay close to you in future, or at least keep an eye on your movements and be ready to come running as soon as it thinks you are about to sneak off and hide.

If there are two of you walking the dog, get your companion to hold the dog's collar or tread on its line while you run ahead. When you stop, turn and call the dog, it should be released. The frustration of being held back should make your dog fly towards you, and when it arrives you can reinforce its delight at reaching you by giving a reward.

It is one thing for an owner to complain that their dog does not respond to them when they call it, but most dogs give their owners an opportunity to communicate and interact many times throughout each walk, but still get ignored. This communication may be subtle, but even a glance in your direction is something you should respond to enthusiastically. Then you should find that your dog becomes attentive and looks at you with increasing frequency, because you are reinforcing the behaviour. The higher level of interaction between you should mean that your dog becomes less likely to go off and do its own thing. Remember, it is important to change the frequency of reinforcement.

Preventing Your Dog From Being A Nuisance To Other People

The public have much higher expectations of dog owners than they used to. This, quite rightly, ranges from expecting dog owners to scoop their dog's poop to intolerance of unruly behaviour. So we need to look at ways of keeping your dog on the straight and narrow.

It is sensible and courteous to keep dogs on a lead in areas where there are large numbers of people walking, playing or sitting in the sun. You have to sympathise with people who are woken from their dosing by a dog licking the sun lotion off their face, or for the families whose beach picnic is raided by hounds from hell. The owners' pathetic restraining calls may prove no bar to the temptations of a child's ice cream when their dog is **100** metres away from them!

154

An obvious way of ensuring that your dog does not run into trouble when it is off the lead is to make sure that it stays close to you by repeatedly calling it, and putting it on a lead before rewarding it and letting it off to go and play again. This will also ensure that your dog does not learn that you only call it to put it on a lead when you see trouble, such as another dog, children, joggers or a horse on the horizon. This is important, because if your dog learns that you only call it to avert a crisis when there is something in the offing, it may scan the horizon to look for interesting trouble when it is called, rather than come back to you.

Down!

One of the trouble-dodging exercises you can teach your dog is the instant '*down!*'. Assuming that your dog already lies down at your signal, the first step is to teach it to lie down wherever it is and whatever it is doing.

Start by getting your dog to lie down at your signal, in your house and garden, making sure that it is taken by surprise as often as possible. For example, tell it to lie down as it dashes past you in the garden or as you pass it in the hall of your house. Over a period of time, gradually increase the distance you are from your dog when you give the signal. When your dog responds, run to it and praise it whilst it is still in the down position to ensure that it receives its reward at the right moment.

Once you have taught your dog to drop to the ground the instant you give the word at home, you can start to practice this exercise in the locations where you walk. As before, gradually increase the distance your dog is from you when you say down, and as soon as it hits the deck, run to it and give it lots of praise. Ultimately you will be able to get your dog to drop into the '*down*' position at great distances from you. Your hard work will be rewarded by the fact that you can drop

155

your dog into the '*down*' position whenever you think it is expedient to do so. For example, if your dog starts to chase a jogger, getting it to lie down may prove to be even more effective than calling it back.

The instant *down!* can also be used if you see a potential problem before your dog does. Once your dog is lying down it will be less likely to react, which will give you a chance to run to it and click its lead on. The instant '*down*' is at its most useful if potential hazards appear between you and your dog, and recalling it is not an option.

Stopping Chase Behaviour That Is Out Of Control

Sometimes the motivation to chase is so strong that it may be necessary to inhibit it before you can develop 'off' training, or reinforce appropriate behaviour. There is no point standing in the middle of a field of rabbits rattling a tin of biscuits in an attempt to stop your dog from chasing the residents if its blood is up and it is excited by the chase. If all else fails, the only way to stop it may be to make it want to avoid rabbits by using training disks as described later in this chapter.

Of course the proper and more obvious way to proceed is to prevent your dog from chasing things, such as sheep, by putting it on a lead. End of problem: all you need is a little common-sense and to be able to anticipate when your dog might be tempted to run off after its potential prey. However there may be times when you cannot predict the problem, for example when joggers suddenly appear in the park. Some dogs are so intent on chasing things that they drag their owners along with them if they are put on a lead, which means that it can be desirable to stop the dog wanting to indulge in chase behaviour in the first place, even if the owner *has* the dog on a lead.

You can put your dog off chasing something by using an aversive experience the sound of a rattle can being thrown to the ground, or conditioned avoidance using training discs. To develop this, start with inanimate objects, such as a toy that is not used for 'retrieve' or 'search' games, to trigger the chase. Roll a toy gently so that it does not move very fast and chase is barely elicited. If your dog moves to chase it, use an aversion or conditioned avoidance technique to interrupt it and pick the toy up while your dog hesitates, so that it is not successful. If your dog does not try and chase, reinforce this with praise, a food reward or another toy from your pocket.

Keep repeating the procedure until it is apparent that your dog has learnt the association between trying to chase the thing that moves and being interrupted in a way it does not like, and then the association between *ignoring* the object it used to chase, and getting a reward. When it keeps choosing the latter you can gradually expose it to more stimulation by making the toy move faster. When you can inhibit your dog's chase behaviour in your home and garden regardless of the amount of stimulation, start working in locations away from home. As before, expose your dog to the minimum amount of stimulation and gradually build up at a pace that is in keeping with its progress. To prevent your dog from having the opportunity to chase something other than your toy that happens to intrude upon your training session - a strolling cat, perhaps - keep your dog on an extending lead or long line (see p. 151).

Sometimes it can be advantageous if a person of the type your dog wants to chase users the aversion/avoidance techniques to put it off, so of course you will have to set this up with volunteers acting as stooges. For example if your dog likes to chase cyclists, you can ask someone to act as a stooge and arm them with the discs, a rattle can or water pistol. When your dog gets to them they can use your selected ammunition to put it off.

It is important that the stooge then remains still until you have been able to get your dog to come back to you. If this is not done, your dog could learn that it is worth persisting, because the fun of the chase will eventually continue.

Once your dog has learnt that any interest in the stimulus results in the aversion/avoidance techniques, while not paying attention to the stimulus results in the arrival of the food reward, and if it has consistently behaved according to plan, you can progress to using the aviodance techniques in situations that occur naturally and combining them with other techniques your dog has learnt, such as '*off*', search games and clicker training.

Search Games

If left to their own devices, dogs would not take exercise for its own sake. Wild dogs and wolves get exercise while travelling in search of prey and during the chase. Obviously, the family dog doesn't need to hunt for its food because we lavish them with regular meals, but its hunting instincts emerge in scavenging and chasing things. We give our dogs exercise for their health, but we also need to provide our dogs with mental stimulation. Occupying your dog's mind and giving it a sense of purpose when it goes for a walk can be an extremely useful way of reducing its interest in things it may want to chase, or of reducing its hostility towards other dogs or people.

You can do this by taking its toys and playing with them and your dog as you walk. If your dog does chase things it should ignore such as cyclists, horses or joggers, it is a good idea to avoid throwing things for it, because this may develop its chase instinct. Search games will exercise some of your dog's hunting drives and give it much more mental stimulation than chasing a ball. Many dogs enjoy these games so much they become intent on waiting for the next game and stick to their owners like glue.

You Will Need:

1. Your dog's favourite toy or a small plastic pot with some holes punched in the lid.

2. Some small food treats, to put in the pot for each game.

3. A cloth or handkerchief.

4. For dogs that have to be kept on a lead: a 7 to 10m rope, or an extending lead attached to its collar.

5. Your dog, any breed, in good health.

6. You - with lots of enthusiasm. Your dog is only going to throw itself into these games if you seem excited about it!

Track Back

Walking on grass or soil leaves a strong trail of scent which is easy for your dog to follow. While keeping your dog on a lead, drop the cloth with some food wrapped in it - without your dog noticing! After a few yards of shuffling your feet to cause as much soil and vegetation disturbance as possible, turn around and slowly walk back towards the cloth, excitedly encouraging your dog to find it - the closer your dog gets, the more excited you must sound.

When your dog reaches the cloth, give it lots of praise and open it to reveal the food which it can then eat. Repeat this exercise at very short distances until your dog understands what the game is all about. It is a bonus if your dog picks up the cloth, but it isn't essential. So long as each game is successful you can progress to using other things with your scent on, working your dog off the lead, and from further distances.

Treasure Hunt

Face an area of grass, with the wind blowing towards you. Holding your dog back, throw or place the toy (or the pot with food in it) just a little in front of you, so that it is just hidden from view. Walk your dog on a lead, zig-zagging from left to right towards the item. Alternatively, you can surreptitiously throw the item into some grass as you walk along when your dog is not looking before starting the exercise.

Because the wind is blowing towards you, and your zig-zag takes you through the path of the scent, your dog should 'find' the item's scent easily. When you notice this has happened, give lots of encouragement and allow your dog to move towards the item. Once your dog finds the 'quarry' you can either have a quick game with the toy, or open the pot and put the food on the ground for it to eat.

Throughout your walks, intermittently charge the pot with some food, taken from a bag carried with you, or use the toy to repeat the process. In time you will be able to stand, facing the area, and encourage your dog to do all the work off the lead. The real challenge comes when you get someone to hide the toy or pot and you and your dog have to find it together.

Hide n' Seek

Some dogs are just not motivated enough to find either toys or food in the form of titbits. You can play the search games for food before your dog's feed time and if necessary use a percentage of its actual diet as the food that is put in the pot for it to find. If your dog still remains unmoved, games of 'hunt the owner' are a good substitute if you have access to suitable terrain. If you are walking on your own, you can take the opportunity to slip away and hide. If more than one person is walking the dog, one can hold it until the other has hidden from view. Either way, when the dog finds the person it is looking for, it should receive lots of praise and perhaps a food treat as well. When your dog has become really proficient, the quarry can hide some time before the dog and handler set out.

Whatever type of game your dog likes to play, you can gradually make it more difficult for your dog to find what it is looking for so that it has to work harder. The results can be very rewarding. Imagine you and your dog being able to find someone, your car keys or something else when you only have a vague idea as to where they might be!

—— 11. ——

An American Revolution: Clicker Training

As you will have noticed, I have concentrated on the importance of training your dog by rewarding and thereby reinforcing appropriate behaviour, as opposed to punishing it every time it puts a foot wrong. Perhaps clicker training is the ultimate illustration of this method.

A revolution went through the American dog training world when dolphin trainer Karen Prior applied the principles of training she had used with dolphins to training dogs. You can use this exciting and enjoyable method to teach any form of trick and response to your wishes that you want to develop.

Clicker training can be combined with lure-reward (see Chapter 5) which will help speed up the rate of progress when you first start developing a response from your dog. You can also use it as an aid to modifying problem behaviour. In fact, after you have developed the few simple exercises discussed here you will only be limited by your imagination and what your dog is physically and behaviourally capable of doing!

The Dolphin Principle

To understand clicker training a little better, try to cast your mind back to any dolphin displays you have seen. You will remember that every so often during the display you heard the sound of a whistle, but you may not remember when you heard it. The whistles are blown when the dolphin is perfoming an exercise (such as a jump), or performing the last part of an exercise sequence - possibly a series of jumps. The dolphin then swims to the side of the pool to receive a fish reward.

This is the principle of what happens: in its early training, a dolphin learns that each time it hears the sound of a whistle it receives a fish. Once this association has been developed, the trainers can use the whistle to reinforce any behaviour the dolphin will perform naturally, and eventually will perform it's task at a given signal. For example, if the trainer wanted to teach the dolphin to jump they could, in theory, wait until the dolphin flopped out of the water of its own volition. When this happened, the trainer would blow the whistle. The association between the sound and food would cause the dolphin to swim to the side of the pool to receive a fish. From then on each time the dolphin performed even the most pathetic flop out of the water it would be rewarded by the sound of the whistle, followed by the provision of a fish when it swam to the side of the pool.

In fine shape

It would not take long for the dolphin to realise that if it swims out into the pool and flops out of the water it can make the whistle go off and earn itself a fish. In other words from the dolphin's point of view it controls the whistle and the supply of fish. However what the trainer is doing is reinforcing an approximation of what is finally required, and this is the start of a process known as **shaping.** Once it was obvious that the dolphin anticipated that the performance of a small flop out of the water elicits the provision of fish, the trainer would withhold the sound of the whistle. The frustration caused by the absence of the anticipated reward would result in the dolphin getting annoyed (for want of a less anthropomorphic expression) and so would try harder, resulting in a slightly more impressive jump. As this is a little closer to the performance the trainer eventually wants, the whistle is blown again and the dolphin gets a fish. Once the dolphin has learnt that a *'flop'* gets nothing, and a small jump makes the whistle go off, the whistle is withheld except for when the dolphin performs a slightly higher jump. This process is repeated until the dolphin eventually achieves those spectacular jumps that delight the crowds .

Signal what you want

Once the dolphin has learnt to perform a jump to make the whistle go off, the trainer can add a signal to trigger the behaviour. For example, if the trainer holds their right arm out when the dolphin swims off to make a jump, the dolphin will learn to swim off and make a jump whenever the trainer repeats that action. In other words, the sight of the trainer holding their arm out allows the dolphin to discriminate between when it can expect to make the whistle go off and get a fish by jumping, and when it can't. This signal is called a discriminating stimulus.

Good dog

You can use a whistle or any sight or other sound to shape your dog's behaviour, even using words like *'Good Dog'*. The trouble is that some sounds or words are inconvenient: we say *'Good Dog'* to our dogs at the wrong time so often, and generally talk to them so much, that it can be difficult for them to know what we are rewarding them for. Enter the humble "clicker", reminiscent of the child's toys that used to be found in Christmas crackers. This is of a convenient size to carry in your pocket and allows you to reward your dog with a novel stimulus that it associates with food, the moment it performs the right action. (Details of where to obtain clickers are on p **283**)

The use of a clicker will teach you to establish the good timing necessary for reinforcing the right behaviour. As we have seen, there is only a half second period for your dog to associate cause and effect. One of the advantages of clicker training is that it is easy to click at the very moment the behaviour occurs, so the dog knows the precise action it is going to get the titbit for. Just as we have seen with the training of dolphins, you will also be able to reward your dog, even at a distance!

First Steps

The first thing to do is to teach your dog that the sound of the clicker is followed by something it likes. The most convenient thing to use is food. If your dog is one of those rare examples that does not get excited about even the most appetising titbit, you may have to use something else, such as a toy.

Sit somewhere with a clicker in your hand. If your dog is scared of noises, use the clicker inside a thick oven glove or similar, and hold it behind your back to muffle the sound for the first few days. Have a pile of titbits next to you, but keep them out of your dog's reach!

Offer a piece of food, and when your dog approaches you, click the clicker a split second before you give it. After a few occasions the time between the click and giving the food can be slowly increased. In every case the click should tell your dog that the food is coming, sometimes almost straight away and sometimes in a moment or two. Once your dog starts to get the idea, throw the titbits to the floor after the sound of the click so that it does not become obsessed with coming to your hand.

Once your dog has associated the click with a titbit, you will want to 'shape' your first behaviour. Let's use 'down' to start with. No doubt your dog can do this, but I want you to see how your dog can learn to trigger the click. Wait patiently until your dog chooses to lie down. When it does, click the clicker, pause, then throw it a titbit. Once you have done this, encourage your dog to move by distracting it, then wait for it to lie down again. You will find that you will not have to repeat this procedure many times before your dog is manipulating the situation by lying down to make the click happen.

Work Harder

Once your dog has got the idea of offering you a down position to get you to click treat and has been doing it well for a few sessions of training, make it work harder and therefore better by not click treating the first time the behaviour is offered. By getting your dog to move, perhaps by moving yourself, you will give it the opportunity to offer the behaviour you want again. When it does, click treat it. Keep it guessing whether it has to do it once, twice or three times to get the click treat. This will make your dog work harder because it will know that if it keeps trying it will succeed. To make sure that your dog always wants to do more, keep it fun, and stick to short training sessions, about five minutes at most.

Unhand Me

To stop an obsession with your feeding hand, you can not only throw the treat to your dog after the click, but also build in a delay between the sound of the click and the giving of the titbit, e.g. by walking to a table to get the titbit after the click, or giving a silent count of five, ten or more before throwing the titbit to the floor. These delays will make it clear to your dog that it is the click, not the titbit, that is the signal of success.

Adding The Signal

Once your dog is working hard for the click-treat and you can anticipate its performance, add the word that will become the signal to tell it what you want it to do to get the click treat. In the example of the down position, your dog will learn to associate the word 'down' with getting down, if you say it every time just before it drops.

Working Longer

Once your dog lies down reliably to earn the click treat when you say the word *'down'*, you can teach it to wait in that position for longer periods to make the click go off. Start with a silent count of five, then build up to ten, and so on. If your dog stays lying down you can give more titbits so that your dog learns that the longer it performs the behaviour the more rewards it can trigger.

Shaping, Reinforcement And Clicking

Technically speaking, the clicker is the **secondary reinforcer** that predicts the **primary reinforcer**, which is food or something else the dog likes. As with other forms of reinforcement, the click-treat technique can be used to shape a behaviour.

167

For example, if your dog is not likely to lie down when you first start, you can click treat it for any action that looks like the beginning of a down movement, such as lowering its head or chest to the ground before it hears the click. You can work towards the down position in incremental stages by gradually making your dog get closer to giving you a full down before you click-treat it.

Here is a good example of how the principle of shaping can be applied, using the click to provide the reinforcement. An Assistance Dog trainer may need to teach a dog to lie on its back on a table so that its future owner, who may have to use a wheelchair, can groom it. There is no point in trying to compel the dog to lie on its back, because the eventual owner will not be able to do so.

Once the dog has learnt to get on the table and lie down in anticipation of a click treat, the trainer withholds the click. When frustrated by this, the dog will either offer other behaviours to elicit the sound of the click, or wait in anticipation of its arrival. Sooner or later it will lean, just slightly, in a direction that would, if the movement was completed, result in it lying on its side or back. When this is observed, the trainer immediately click-treats it. The trainer waits until the movement is performed again before reinforcing with a click-treat, and so on, until the dog realises that leaning causes the click.

As described above in getting a dog to lie down, the trainer begins to withhold the click to make the dog try a little harder by leaning further to one side, which earns a click-treat. By degrees, the dog learns that to trigger the click it has to roll onto its side and eventually onto its back. Once this is achieved the trainer can add the word or other signal that tells the dog when to roll and keep it waiting a little bit longer each time so that it remains in position.

Try this game which is an exercise in shaping:

Put a small mat or hand towel sized cloth on the floor. Each time your dog steps near it, click, then treat. Move the mat every so often to make sure your dog is learning to focus on it. Once your dog gets the idea, only click-treat when it stands on it and finally only when it lies on it, using the technique for shaping a down if necessary. Then add the word 'mat' each time your dog lies on the mat, and build up the time it has to stay there to get the click-treat. Don't get frustrated if it takes time for your dog to get the idea; it will, sooner or later. In the mean time just enjoy watching it work out the problem. As a bonus, once you have both mastered the exercise you can take the mat or towel wherever you visit knowing that when you spread it out your dog will lie on it.

Will I Have To Use The Clicker Forever?

Understandably, the thought that you might be tied to the clicker may seem a little off-putting, but this is not the case. Consider the clicker as a method of teaching a new behaviour or establishing a previously learned behaviour in new or difficult circumstances. When the objective of establishing the behaviour has been met, the clicker can be gradually faded out. For example, once your dog is reliable at performing a specific action when you say 'down' or 'sit' to make the click-treat happen, you can start to phase out the clicker and use the reinforcement techniques of praise and titbits as discussed in chapter 5. However if you then want your dog to perform the same behaviour in crowded conditions, or want to teach something new, you should dust off your clicker and arm yourself with rewards.

Problem Solving

Clicker training has great potential as a means of reinforcing appropriate behaviour in the treatment of behaviour problems. Let's look again at the common problem of a dog's tendency to get over-excited in the presence of visitors to the home. You can ask your visitors to ignore your dog's advances and wait patiently until your dog gives up and lies down. When it does, reward it with a click-treat. The click-treats can continue at intervals while your dog remains lying down, but they should stop when your dog gets up and moves. It won't take long for your dog to work out that it is better off if it stays lying down in these circumstances!

You can use a similar approach if your dog has a tendency to pull on the lead. Whenever those moments of walking near your side occur, reward your dog with a click-treat. This will increase the likelihood of it walking by your side so that it can get another click-treat. Then you can gradually shape its behaviour until it is walking right next to you to get the clicks.

If your dog becomes a little excited when it sees other dogs whilst it is on a lead, wait until it looks away from the other dog, sniffs the ground or better still looks at you, and give a click-treat. Similarly, if your dog barks excessively when people walk past your house you can increase the frequency of quieter behaviour by click-treating your dog when it does not bark at the sounds outside your home.

The modification of some behaviours requires the dog to be relaxed, and therefore it is relaxed behaviour that will be reinforced by the click-treat. As a result the dog's emotional state as well as its behaviour will be altered. This can be very beneficial in some situations. If your dog is a little nervous of visitors, make the sound of the click each time your dog looks relaxed, at the sound of which your visitor can drop a titbit on the floor.

Sometimes treatment of a problem requires the training of a behaviour that is incompatible with what your dog's normal response would be. Let's use the example of the dog that steals tissues, then disappears under a table and guards them. The dog can be taught to go to its bed when it hears 'bed' - using the method described above for teaching it to go to its mat - to get a click-treat. Then, when the dog steals something, it should be possible say 'bed' and cause the dog to abandon the item because it has gone to its bed to trigger the click-treat, thereby completely removing any hint of conflict.

— 12. —

Dominance

Feeding Rituals.

Today, somewhere in the Arctic tundra, the breath of a wolf pack will be puffing like smoke in the frozen air as they stealthily approach their prey, their eyes searching for clues that will tell them which of the musk oxen is the easiest to catch- a limp, or signs of lethargy will give the game away. It is more likely they will separate one of the young from the rest of the group. In a final rush, the wolves will stampede the herd and, if they are lucky, they will succeed in bringing down the food they need to survive.

The dominant male and female take over the carcass and defend it from the rest of the pack. Body language plays an important role in preventing actual conflict. The rest of the pack slink submissively around the carcass displaying the food begging behaviour seen in young cubs, until the dominant pair have had their fill.

Meanwhile, at home, Jason the Golden Retriever barks demandingly at the cupboard where the food is kept because it is time to be fed. Obediently, Mum stops preparing the family meal and opens a tin, empties it with some mixer into a bowl and puts it down for him.

Many of the people bitten by dogs each year are bitten by their own pet, or one that is well known to them. A frequent cause for this is the fact that the dog has been allowed to develop a sense of being a dominant member of the family-pack.

You used to hear dog trainers up and down the land suck on their teeth, the way car mechanics do when they are about to tell you the bad news, and say "that's a dominant dog" as if the owner's cherished pet had popped out of the womb that way. It has become fashionable to challenge the concept of the dominant dog. Those dominant dogs are still there of course; what has been called into question is how they became dominant in the first place.

A truly dominant or high ranking dog is not necessarily what people think it is. In the **1970**'s, research conducted by Dr. Ian Dunbar [1] clearly showed that the dogs likely to show aggressive behaviour in status or pecking order disputes are middle ranking. Most of the time these displays are nothing more than posturing in situations where they feel threatened.

Dogs that are truly dominant are confident in their ability to take or keep what they want and make little fuss about it, but on the rare occasions that assertion is necessary, their put-downs are firm. Our dogs' ancestors evolved a pecking order because this reduces conflict, and saves unnecessary energy and the risk of injury, all of which would reduce hunting efficiency and the likelihood of survival. The reduction in conflict is achieved because each individual knows where its stands in the group.

However, relationships are not straightforward and there are many variables in each dog-to-dog and dog-to-person combination. This variation is caused by three factors.[2] Imagine for a moment that you are a dog walking towards another. It has got food. Do you want to try and get it? The three things to consider are:

1. What has been your previous relationship with this dog? Have you or it been a pushover or are the honours even?

2. Is the food worth having? There may be a big difference between its desire to guard (and your desire to get) a chocolate bar and a bowl of cold porridge, but this depends upon how you feel about cold porridge, and how hungry you are.

3. Are you going to get hurt? Even if the other dog has lost out to you in the past, it is currently in possession of the food and you have got to get close enough to take it away.

If you think you can win, you really want the food and you've got nothing to lose - go ahead and take it. If you are right the other dog will predict it will come off worse, if it challenges you and will give way, unconsciously indicating the fact that it lacks the confidence to challenge you in its body language.

Whatever a dog's capacity to become a bossy boots, a sense of ability to actually become one has to be learnt. This is achieved by observing the signals of other members of the group, and remembering the outcome of interactions with them.

The signals that dogs get from other pack members tend to be genuine and, although often subtle, unambiguous. However within the family (the dog's adoptive pack), the wrong signals are sometimes given which can lead to relationship problems. Think of the example above and ask yourself, if you are a dog with a bone will you give it to another dog? If you do, is that dog more or less likely to think you are weaker than it is? If it thinks you are weaker is it more likely to throw its weight around and challenge you in other situations?

Now let's put the questions in a family context. If you are wandering about the house with a piece of toast and you break some off and give it to your dog, is it going to see you as a stronger member of the pack or a weaker one? If the answer is weaker, is your dog now more or less likely to challenge you in other situations?

Relationship problems can arise when we forget the canine perspective as a pack animal, and give it signals that it interprets as subordinate or weak. These signals may make the dog think it enjoys a higher status than the family it lives with. This can result in a dog in conflict with other members of the family, because their expectations of the dog's behaviour are not consistent with the way they interact with it.

As a result, the dog does not know where it stands, which can be very stressful. This stress may make the dog more reactive and inclined to aggression. Although dominance aggression is a term often used to describe the problems that can occur within a household, we should really think of the aggression part as something that occurs as a result of the dominance system breaking down.

"But Hey!" you cry, "I give my dog bits of my toast all the time and it doesn't have a dominance problem!" Well no, you probably don't have a problem because relationships are not that straightforward.

For example, a truly dominant dog may let another dog share or even take its bone because it still 'owns it' and knows it can take it back any time it wants. In short, another dog's interest in the food does not make it feel threatened. You may be similarly permissive and will not feel threatened if children from within your social circle take possession of something you consider to be yours.

If you are in the habit of regularly sharing your toast with your dog there are probably rules that you enforce when you want to, as a result of which your dog knows that when you want something to happen it has to comply, so you must be top dog despite sharing your toast. These rules work, provided they are enforced when you want them to be, and that they are about issues important to your dog.

You also have to consider that although the worst cases in this category can eventually result in someone being bitten, a dog's dominant demeanour does not necessarily mean it will be aggressive; in fact, in most cases it isn't. But a dog's sense of high status can lead it to be reluctant to come when called, or to obey your other wishes. It can lead to many problems, such as an excessive level of attention-seeking behaviour (although poor responses and attention-seeking behaviour are not necessarily related to dominance), an over-developed sense of responsibility for guarding the territory or itself if it is frightened, and even excessive pulling on the lead.

Are You The Leader Of Your Pack?

Try enforcing the following rules to see if you are the leader of your pack, but before you start, note that you are not allowed to touch your dog. If you already know that the answer is no, or try the exercises and discover to your amazement that you are not Leader of the Pack, don't get annoyed with your dog, but recognise that it needs more rules so it can understand where it stands. (N.B. You must be sure it knows how to respond before you ask it to do something. Also do not try and take food from your dog because you may cause the development of defensive behaviour you don't want (see p 219).

1. Let your dog up onto the couch and let it settle down. Now tell it to get off again. Does it do it?

2. Let your dog onto your bed and repeat the exercise above. Have you got your bed back?

3. Will your dog step back and let you go through doors first?

4. Will your dog get out of your way when you tell it to?

5. Can you send your dog out of the room you are sitting in or prevent it from entering the room until you are ready, without closing the door?

6. If you are eating, will your dog go away and lie down if you tell it to?

7. Will your dog let you win the games you play with toys if you seem determined?

8. Make some of your own rules and see if your dog responds as you want it to. Does it?

If the answer to all of these is yes, well done. Remember that it is important to test these frequently to make sure nothing has changed.

If you think you need to introduce more rules, these guidelines should help you choose some that are appropriate:

Think again about the example of you eating a piece of toast. If you don't hand it over, you will convey your higher status. This can be enhanced further if you tell your dog to go away when it shows interest in your food. There are many other signals we can give our dogs to confer a more appropriate status upon them, but we do not have to be harsh or bullying. The techniques can be very subtle and may seem to be unimportant at the time; but remember the maxim, 'If you look after the pennies the pounds will look after themselves'.

Some owners report that their dogs look subdued when they first introduce some rules. This can occur because of the dog's response to experiences that are not consistant with its expectations. Once it has made a mental adjustment to the new regime, it will settle down again.

You can make it clear to your dog that you are in control by telling it to comply with a request first so that it "earns" its reward. For example, you may tell it to sit before you stroke it if it is seeking attention, or before it is allowed onto the sofa. These variations on a theme are not contradictory, because the application of the rules is on a sliding scale. How you impose them is dependent upon what seems necessary, which you can only judge from your dog's behaviour.

Prior to maturity however, dogs will not necessarily show the consequences of receiving the wrong signals from the group it lives with. It is a good idea to test its response to your wishes very frequently, as discussed above, or to apply the rules below until your dog has grown up, and you are sure that it knows what the boundaries are. Whatever your dog's age, concentrate on the rules that seem important to it:

Rule 1

Do not feed your dog food from your plate, or while you are eating.

Reason

So that you do not seem to be a subordinate that gives up its food. This will also make it less likely that your dog will be interested in trying to get your food at other times, and therefore less likely that it will take food you do not want it to have, or start scrounging when you are eating.

Rule 2

Always feed your dog after you have had your meal. If you are not going to eat until later, sit down and have a cup of tea or something after preparing your dog's food, thus making it wait until you are ready.

Reason

Make it seem that you have first share.

Rule 3

Do not let your dog into the bedrooms or upstairs; but don't use a child gate or other barrier to bar its access. Use your personality and presence to achieve the objective. It does not matter that your dog tries to go upstairs, it is important that it leaves when you tell it to.

Reason

Regard these areas as your den into which you will not allow your dog.

Rule 4

Sometimes stand in your dog's bed or make it move away from its favourite resting place and occupy it.

Reason

This lets your dog know you have the ability to go anywhere you want and to claim its areas for yourself.

Rule 5

Do not let your dog sit on the furniture or on your lap.

Reason

A dog is more likely to perceive itself as having a high status if it can occupy the highest level and impose itself on others. You can see the importance of height if you think of how our own society has developed. In a court of law the judge sits in the highest place; at the state opening of parliament the Queen sits in the highest place and in a cathedral the bishop sits in the highest place. These are all ritualizations of hierarchical structure in our own society, although it is questionable whether in the dog's view of things, height for its own sake is important. It is more likely to value sitting in your favourite chair, or lap, because it is more comfortable! From a status point of view it does not matter that your dog hops on the furniture when you are not present. What is important is that it hops off when you reappear.

Rule 6

Groom your dog daily whether it needs it or not.

Reason

Imposing yourself on your dog in this way will reinforce your status.

Rule 7

Do not allow your dog to successfully demand attention. Give it affection on your initiative. Call it to you.

Reason

Dominant pack members tend to be aloof to approaches made by subordinates.

Rule 8

Make sure your dog gives way to you at doorways.

Reason

Dominant dogs precede subordinates. Significantly, conflict over who goes through the door first often develops when two dogs or bitches living in the same household start to have fights. This may be because which one goes first is an issue in itself or because the doorway brings them in to close proximity. The behaviour of a pack of hounds as their kennel door was opened was once filmed many times in succession. Each time the top hound came through the door first.

Rule 9

Do not step over or walk around your dog: make it move.

Reason

Subordinate dogs defer to dominant dogs.

Rule 10

When walking your dog on or off the lead, frequently change direction without warning. If you only have a straight path to walk on retrace your steps every so often.

Reason

This makes it clear that you determine the pace and direction of travel. If you always use the same routes, and most of us do most of the time, it may seem to your dog that it is leading the pack because you seem to trot along behind as it anticipates the route.

Social Isolation

The dog is a social animal, and needs the company of other members of the group it lives with. Contact and interaction will be very important to your dog, and if you eject it from the group, it will want to return. Denying it the opportunity to do so will make a statement about your status in the group.

For example, if you are sitting in a room with your dog, you can tell it to leave. Do not shut the door, because this will defeat the object of teaching the dog to respond to your personality. Each time your dog tries to step over the threshold of your room, send it back out again. Once you feel the dog has accepted that it cannot re-enter until you say so, you will have made your point, and you can call it back into the room when you are ready.

Games

Play games and win. Playing games with toys simulates different types of hunting behaviour and competition between pack members. Of course dogs do not visualise hunting when they play, but playing stimulates the built-in patterns of hunting behaviour dogs have inherited. There are three categories of game:

Chase Games

Chasing a ball activates the same instincts as chasing a rabbit or other prey.

Killing Games

Shaking a toy simulates the kill. Squeaky toys are favourites because they make the same sort of sounds as a dying animal. Very often, once the squeak comes out the dog loses interest because it is 'dead'.

Possession Games

Tug-of-war games imitate ripping a carcass apart, and the battle for the best of the meat. Running around with a toy and not letting other members of the 'pack', or family have possession of it simulates retaining the prize of the hunt.

The type of game your dog favours is likely to vary according to his or her breed type. For example, Bull Terriers were bred and kept for baiting, consequently they have a preference for tug-of-war games. There are some dogs that do not show an interest in toys at all and will be quite happy to watch you go charging up and down the garden in pursuit of a rubber ring without feeling the need to join in. Sometimes this is due to a lack of opportunity to learn how to play in early life. Obviously there is no point trying to play to make a point if your dog is not interested.

Games with toys not only act out hunting behaviour, they also provide an opportunity for competition and establishing roles and status, without any conflict. By playing games with your dog or puppy and winning them yourself, you can make a statement about your status that is subtle in implementation, but dramatic in its effect. The more you win games to convey your capacity to hang onto the prize, the more likely you are to maintain the appropriate status quo.

The routine outlined below can be highly successful in helping to establish and maintain you as number one in the pecking order.

It's important your dog does not have a box full of toys it regards as some sort of trophy cabinet to help itself from whenever it wants. So pick up all your dog's toys and put them away, out of its reach. They are now your toys. (Chews and bones do not count as toys and can be left down, but never use them as toys. Of course you will leave the interactive key on the floor if you are using it. See page 123) The rules of these games are not to be confused with the search games discussed on page 158 and should be seen as a separate exercise). Follow this simple four stage process and play as often as possible each day. The frequency depends upon your dog's level of interest, of course.

Stage One

Start by getting a toy out and inviting your dog to play. Initiating the game is a reversal of roles if your dog has been in the habit of trotting up to you and dropping a toy on your lap or at your feet, as if to say, 'Hoi! you! Yes you, couch potato, play!'

Play energetically for a while, allowing your dog to win, and generally enjoy the game to the full.

Stage Two

While your dog is still enthusiastic about the game, start playing to win. For example, in chase games, throw the toy and get there first, or in tug-of-war games, gain possession of the toy. No, I'm not asking the impossible. Cheat!

When playing chase games, for example, you can throw the toy a short distance after conning your dog into going in the wrong direction. You can cheat at tug-of-war with a sneaky squirt from a water pistol which will normally cause the dog to let go of the toy. Whatever your means of ensuring success, your dog should start to realise it is up against a real competitor. Repeat the winning process a few times in each game to ensure you've made your point. If you cannot win tug-of-war games convincingly, do not play them at all. Avoid teaching your dog to become confident about getting physical with you.

Stage Three

Play with the toy by yourself and deny your dog any opportunity to regain possession, while continuing to stimulate its interest in the game. For example, with two or more family members you can play 'piggy in the middle' accidentally (on purpose) dropping the toy from time to time and then diving on it to regain possession. Alternatively, two people can play tug-of-war, and when your dog tries to join in you can tell it to go away. If you're on your own, you can throw the toy from hand to hand, guarding it jealously.

The point of the exercise is to keep your dog excited and competitive and then mildly challenge it, to retain the toy yourself. However the all important trick is to find the balance between asserting yourself by winning and ensuring your dog enjoys itself.

Stage Four

End each game before your dog gets bored, but don't just throw the toy down and walk away. If you do your dog can pick it up and it will have won after all. Instead, you should jubilantly put the toy away again. It is hoped that by playing games in this way, your dog will see you as a winner, not a wimp, a member of the group to respect and make it feel secure, rather than someone to disregard in other situations.

Ensuring Peace And Harmony If The Family Includes Another Dog Or Dogs

Aggression between two dogs in the same household is, in my experience, the hardest of all behaviour problems to cure, except the problem of bitches that fight. As someone who has seen some severe cases of fighting between dogs or bitches that live in the same household, I have perhaps too jaundiced a view! There are lots of dogs of the same gender living together in perfect harmony, including my own. However, the ability to avoid problems developing should be high on every owner's list of priorities, because severe injury, death or rehoming are all possible outcomes if the problem starts. Living with two dogs that fight on sight and keeping them separated is possible, but the stress of trying to remember to keep all the doors shut is enough to make anyone go prematurely grey.

The potential for cohabiting dogs to fight is increased by the artificial environment in which we make them live. Naturalists have filmed a she wolf chasing a rival for five miles before being content she was off her territory and no longer a threat. However, resolving differences in this fashion tends to be impossible in the average living room. Although we should not draw direct comparisons with our dogs and the wolf because of the dog's neotenisation, a drive to eliminate or subjugate a rival can emerge in extreme cases.

Aggression between a dog and a bitch that live in the same household occurs more rarely than aggression between dogs of the same sex, age, size or temperament, when it may be more difficult for them to establish a pecking order. If their similarity seems to be the only motivation for aggression, there is, in my experience, little that owners can do to improve the situation, particularly if fighting occurs when the two are left to their own devices. It's perhaps wise to avoid buying litter brothers and sisters who will obviously be very similar to each other as their blood ties will not be a bar to aggression.

If two bitches or two dogs must be owned, it is sensible to select individuals that contrast as much as possible in terms of age, size and temperament. One way of increasing the social gap between potential rivals is to identify the one which shows more subordinate behaviour, and to consult your vet about neutering it. Neutering the subordinate male or female can reduce its competitiveness, and make it seem less of a rival. Aggressive behaviour between bitches can be made worse, or triggered, if it is hormonally driven. In this case the problems will occur around the time of their season and during false pregnancy. If a bitch is aggressive specifically at the time of her season, neutering should be considered. (Also see Chapter 18)

Inappropriate Owner Interference

Fortunately, in a substantial number of cases, it is the owner's tendency to upset the status quo that is the cause of status disputes, and significantly there are no fights when the owners are absent, because the dogs have worked out their own pecking order. In many cases it is clear which dog should be dominant, but the owners want to treat them as equals, or they feel sorry for the subordinate who is always being 'picked on' and make a fuss of it. Sometimes the owners want to elect the oldest dog or the one with longest residency as the dominant individual, because in their view it is the right thing to do.

These are all natural emotions driven by a sense of caring for our dogs as pets and sharing our lives with them. We bring to this relationship our own set of values, but dogs are likely to perceive the situation very differently. The dominant dog may perceive the other as taking liberties, because it cannot understand that the subordinate dog is actually being singled out for privileges. As a result it may try to re-establish the pecking order.

This in turn may stimulate yet more preferential treatment for the subordinate dog, or determined even-handedness from the owners, and so a vicious circle develops. Furthermore, the increased number of attacks suffered by the subordinate may cause it to become defensive, and eventually it may initiate incidents of aggression in anticipation of being attacked, especially if it feels that the owner is on its side.

Although there can be a sudden onset of aggression, owners often report that problems develop over a period. At first, they become aware of increased competition over things that did not seem to matter before. Fundamentally these tend to be those prizes and privileges identified in the rules mentioned earlier. An important addition to this list of privileges is access to the owners. (See Jealousy p 258).

Role Reversal

What should be done to establish and maintain the appropriate status quo? Quite simply, the roles have to be reversed. Despite our human sympathies, we have to ignore the subordinate as much as possible, giving favour and privilege instead to the higher ranking dog. For example, the owner should pet the higher ranking dog while ignoring the subordinate one when they are both present.

This may be hard to accept but the subordinate may be more relaxed because it is not being put on the spot all the time. The dominant dog should be fed first, put on the lead first- in fact, be first in everything. Exceptions to this rule can occur if it is apparent that the dog with higher status does not value the resources of the owner's attention, etc. or is preventing the other from entering the owner's car or house, once it is in a position to defend it. In these situations it may be beneficial to put the subordinate in first.

Often the subordinate dog is picked up, cuddled and comforted after an altercation, while the dominant one is confronted with all sorts of punishment - a certain recipe for it to want to re-establish itself at the next opportunity. Instead, once the dogs are separated and the dominant one restrained, the subordinate should be told to go away. This action will help to reinforce the top dog's status. Of course this will not be practical if the situation has deteriorated to the point where serious fighting occurs. At this point, professional help will be needed (see p 281).

The owner's role in these pack dynamics goes beyond helping to reinforce the dogs' hierarchy. The dogs' perception of their owners' position is just as important. Observations of wolf packs have shown that if the alpha members are firmly established at the top of the hierarchical ladder, there is little fighting in the lower orders. Similarly, if the owners are clearly dominant over the dogs living in their household, the chances of the dogs fighting each other for pole position are much reduced, and displays of aggression become inhibited by the owner's presence.

Introducing A New Dog

To avoid problems when introducing a new dog, or when one comes to visit, the dogs should meet away from home, preferably on neutral territory. Unvaccinated puppies will be restricted to the garden, but adult dogs and adolescents can be walked together. By the time they arrive at the resident dog's home, they will have had a chance to become accustomed to each other and will have started to establish a relationship - provided, of course, that neither one has a problem mixing with other dogs generally.

Frustrated Play

Owners frequently introduce a new puppy into the household to rejuvenate an older dog, and to soften the blow when their older companion has died. The older dog also teaches the younger the routines. This is good practice, but it is worth being aware that if not handled correctly, things can go wrong. The puppy will pose no threat to its older companion until it is mature, but once it reaches maturity it may challenge the older dog for the chief perks of the household.

Once the hierarchy starts to shift, dominance issues which never seemed to matter before, such as who goes through the door first, or the possession of toys or food, can take on a new significance, gradually becoming the focus for minor disagreements. As days go by, serious aggression can develop.

Difficulties can also arise if the older dog or bitch is inhibited by its owner's presence and allows a puppy to take liberties it would not normally get away with. The maturing puppy is then convinced that the older dog is a pushover. If, after initial acceptance, dog and puppy are left to their own devices, the puppy is more likely to develop a healthy respect for its older companion, which may also inhibit it from trying to take over as the months go by.

The phenomenon of younger dogs learning to mouth and pull at older dogs can also result in the youngster learning that the way to interact with other dogs generally is to bite and pull at them, particularly in play. If the dogs it subsequently meets take exception to this and are aggressive towards it, the youngster can become inclined to aggressive behaviour towards dogs in meets away from home either because it anticipates a confrontation or because of the frustration generated because it cannot rush up and greet them in this overly physical way.

Scent Marking

We have already noted that communication by scent is very important to the dog. In the wild, male wolves scent-mark territorial boundaries. This is mostly done by urinating in prominent places. The same behaviour is common in male dogs. It may be that the behaviour is not triggered by territorial marking as such, but is stimulated where a dog or wolf feels insecure. In the wild the fact that the scent is present tells approaching groups of wolves that others are in the vicinity and they avoid the territory, or at least avoid going far into it. Of course dogs do not have the opportunity to avoid areas that have been scent-marked by others because we walk them straight through them.

Scent-marking behaviour seems to be most frequent in dogs that have been allowed to develop a sense of high status within their family/pack, despite a lack of confidence. One of the ways that can help to reduce this perception of dominance is not allowing your dog to scent-mark on every lamp post and tree when you are walking it on a lead.

Instead, keep it walking with an attitude of "this is my walk that you are on, not vice-versa, so I am not waiting for you to investigate where other dogs have been or letting you leave your calling card behind." This will not be possible when your dog is off the lead of course, but nonetheless, keep moving rather than appearing to stand by patiently while your dog carries out the anointing process.

It is worth noting that it is often easier to start to cure a dog's aggression towards other dogs in areas that it is not used to. Why this should be, is unclear. Perhaps these areas are not associated with fear or conflict, or the dog in question is inhibited by the presence of the scent of dogs it is not familiar with, or it does not feel secure enough about showing aggression because it has not had the opportunity to leave its own scent yet. Or even a combination of these factors!

Scent-marking is also related to sexual behaviour. The presence of scent left behind by a bitch in season will not only stimulate male dogs to investigate the smell and try and find her, it will also stimulate them to leave urine marks in the vicinity. You may also find that your dog keeps turning round and returning to the place where her scent is and that it will salivate slightly and even gnash its teeth. (Also see neutering p 274)

NOTES

1.   Dunbar I. Dog Behaviour   T.F.H. Publications Inc. (1979) POB 427, Neptune, New Jersey, USA

2.   Wickens, S. *Lecture on Dominance: How does it develop and how do people fit in* Given at the Association of Pet Behaviour Councilors Symposium 1994 presented by Bradshaw, J. (published in APBC proceedings 1994)

——— 13. ———

Fears and Phobias

You may be lucky enough to have a dog that is not fazed by any of the experiences that life throws at it, however dramatic or traumatic they may be. However it is more likely that it will be affected in some ways, either by a bad experience, or by a lack of experience.

Dogs that seem to be confident can take us by surprise by reacting to something unusual, such as someone standing in a manhole (dogs are not used to seeing people cut off at the waist). The range of reaction to novel and challenging stimuli varies from caution (a healthy response) to suspicion and even to running away in extreme circumstances. Where flight is denied - if the dog is on a lead, for example - fear aggression may develop (see Chapter 15). How we react to our dog's fear affects how they will respond in future, and to know how best to deal with these situations it helps to have some idea about your dog's nervous system.

It will help to simplify things by thinking of this as functionally divided into two halves. One half is called the Sympathetic Autonomic Nervous System and the other half is called the Parasympathetic Autonomic Nervous System. If we remove the jargon we can interpret these as arousal (sympathetic) and relaxation (parasympathetic). The arousal effect includes increased heart rate, increased respiration, increased bowel movement (sometimes resulting in loss of toilet control), plus the chemical reactions we know as sensations and recognise as emotional states such as fear, anxiety or aggression. As you would expect, the relaxation side of the nervous system has the opposite effect.

Our own nervous system, just like a dog's, also has mutually exclusive actions. For example, when feeling very anxious we lose our appetite. If we fear that a loved one has been involved in an accident we cannot put our feet up and watch the television. Instead we pace backwards and forwards, peering through the curtains and willing the phone to ring.

When some dogs are left unattended they will not eat the chews or biscuits they have been left with, however fresh they are and despite the fact that in any other circumstances they would have eaten them straight away. This is because they are anxious about their owner's absence. Relaxation is overridden, and appetite is lost. Significantly, the dog will eat the biscuits or chews as soon as the owner returns home.

The incompatibility of the two halves of the system has evolved so that the body shuts down what it does not need at a time of crisis. For example, if you lived in the wild you would not be inclined to put your feet up or stop to eat if there was a tiger in the bush next to you. Instead your body would gear up to fight or run away, your heart would be pounding in your chest and your breath would become short and fast. Those prehistoric animals that went on displaying relaxed behaviour whenever their lives were at risk like this didn't last long enough to pass on their genes to the next generation. Conversely, those animals that over-reacted to everything around them were not best suited for survival either, because they wasted too much time and energy reacting to things that were not a threat.

Change The Behaviour - Change The Emotions

One of the reasons why we need to be aware of the two halves of the nervous system is that behaviour is the expression of emotions. To change our dog's behaviour, we need to alter its emotional state. For example, a dog might hear thunder in the distance, which makes it nervous. The active side of its nervous system builds up. Perhaps the dog begins to pace about, pant and shake. It may then try to find somewhere where it feels more secure, such as at the back of the smallest room in the house, in a cupboard, under its owner's bed or behind some furniture. At this point, if the owner tries to reassure the dog, he will have the effect of praising it for being frightened - which will reinforce its fear. The dog cannot understand the words used for comfort or reassurance, but the attention it gets increases the likelihood that it will react fearfully the next time thunder is heard. It is also likely that the extent of the dog's reaction will increase.

Happily this process also works in reverse! For example, if your dog is nervous at the sight or sound of something, such as heavy traffic, you can alter its behaviour and therefore its emotional response by ignoring any signs of distress when you are in the vicinity of heavy traffic. When it seems to be relaxed, give it pats and attention. This will reinforce relaxation, making it more likely to occur when you are near heavy traffic on future occasions.

Counter-Conditioning

As discussed above, if you are anxious you cannot eat, but if you are eating you must be relaxed. So if your dog does not react to the sound of a heavy lorry going past and you give it a tit bit or produce its favourite toy from your pocket, it will relax even more. In this way an association between the presence of lorries and relaxation can be built up. This approach can be combined with clicker training (see Chapter 11) to provide a more accurate means of reinforcing relaxed behaviour.

However, if you throw an anxious dog in at the deep end, it will be too scared to eat or show interest in its toy and there will be no opportunity for you to reinforce relaxed behaviour. To prevent this happening you must very slowly build up your dog's exposure to the experiences that frighten it. For example, if a sound is the problem, you can start by making a recording of the sound and playing it at such a low level that anxiety is not induced. The following procedure should be carried out each day, preferably on a little and often basis.

Sit with your dog on a lead and feed it its diet by hand on a piecemeal basis. The delivery of each piece of food should immediately follow each rise in, or occurrence of, the sound your dog is frightened of, so that the sound becomes the clue that predicts food. When it becomes apparent that your dog anticipates food each time the sound occurs you can gradually increase the volume. Progress very slowly, perhaps over several weeks or even months if necessary, to avoid any setbacks.

Once your dog is able to relax even when the recorded sound is loud, you can progress to using the real stimulus. You should, however, be at such a distance from the sound that anxiety is not elicited; for example, if lorries are the problem, you can stand a long distance from the main road. Some owners have regularly found themselves standing two or three fields away from home with a child's cap gun in their hand, while their partner remains at home with the dog, ready to counter-condition the dog's fear of gunfire by giving it food each time the cap gun goes off. To further minimise the sound, the doors and windows of the house are closed. As the dog makes progress, the distance between it and the source of the sound will be reduced - but never to the point where the noise can reverberate inside the house, as the sound may be too great.

The following case history (with name changed) will help to illustrate the main points of counter-conditioning.

One morning, Gemma, a six year old black Labrador, was being walked by her retired owner along a footpath that ran along the edge of a large school playing field, where rugby practise was taking place. Suddenly a stray ball hurtled towards them and hit the unsuspecting Gemma on the head with a resounding thump, which caused her to panic. Her owner's understandable response was to reassure her, and to try and stop her frantically pulling backward on the extending lead. Eventually Gemma recovered enough to be able to continue her walk.

When they approached the same location, the next day, Gemma became anxious and wanted to stop. Her owner tried to reassure her and encourage her to keep moving, and was eventually successful. On each successive day Gemma stopped at the same location, and each time it took her owner longer to persuade her to start walking again. On each occasion Gemma looked more frightened, and she became even more frightened when her owner tried to reassure her. The situation deteriorated quickly. By the end of the first week Gemma not only stopped where she had been hit by the ball, but also pulled in the direction of home if she heard a game in progress, or the sound of the referee's whistle. In the end her owner had no choice but to give up and follow her.

If the problem had stopped there, Gemma's owner could have worked around it by using a different route. But this was not to be, because Gemma started to respond fearfully to the sound of the referee's whistles on television. By the time her owner was aware that the sound was triggering the fear, Gemma had also become conditioned to respond fearfully whenever she heard the roar of a crowd, coming from the television. This development occurred because the noise was associated with the sound of the whistle. Two weeks after the original incident, any sports programme that involved the sound of a whistle or a crowd would cause Gemma to run into her owner's bedroom and hide under the dressing table. In this refuge, she shook uncontrollably and salivated copiously whilst receiving her owner's reassurance.

This story illustrates how fear of something specific can be triggered by things which are associated with it. In the same way that Pavlov conditioned his dogs to salivate when they heard a metronome because it was associated with food, fear can be triggered by things that predict the event that causes it. In Gemma's case this was shown when her fear was triggered by experiences associated with the footpath where she had been hit by the ball. Pavlov also reported that a Dr. Frolov taught dogs to associate the sight of a black square with the metronome that caused salivation and eventually he was able to trigger salivation with the square alone. This is a phenomenon referred to as **second order conditioning**. In Gemma's case this was the sound of a referee's whistle. She then became fearful when she heard the sound of crowds, because this was associated with the sound of the whistle.

Another case showed this mechanism quite well. A German Shepherd Dog that had received insufficient habituation in early life became fearful of passing traffic. It did not mind travelling in its owner's car, because this was only associated with short trips deeper into the countryside for a walk. One day, a change in circumstances meant that the owner had to take his dog to work in the car and encounter the rush hour traffic which so frightened the dog. This resulted in the dog becoming fearful of entering its owner's car because it predicted the experience of the traffic. Finally, the dog became fearful when it heard the sound of the owner's car keys, because of its association with getting in the car.

The triggers for the dog's fear generalised when it became too frightened to get into the car belonging to the owner's girlfriend, even though it had never been taken on busy roads in it. A typical example of generalisation for fear of sounds is: fear of fireworks, which progresses to fear of guns or bird scarers, then even on to sticks spitting in the hearth. In one case this process went on to include the sound of a child proof lock on a medicine bottle going 'click'.

Owner Reinforcement

If we look again at Gemma's story, we can see that the key to the development of the problem lies in the owner's attempts to reassure her. After the initial incident, Gemma's owner tried to comfort her, using a sympathetic voice. It may have seemed to Gemma that her

199

owner's wimpy noises were her own reaction to the same event because she could not understand the definition of the words she used. More importantly, her owner's attention made it seem as if she was being praised for being frightened. This reinforcement increased the sensation of fear Gemma felt when she saw the path or heard the sounds. Ultimately Gemma did not have to be hit with the football again for the problem to develop further, because the sensation of her own fear became the unpleasant event that followed the sound of the whistle, and her owner's attention helped this reinforcement process along.

How could the problem have been prevented?

As far as possible the owner should have ignored Gemma's fearful behaviour when she was hit by the ball, and rewarded her as soon as she had recovered. When Gemma stopped walking on the day after the incident, her owner should have continued to walk to the end of the lead. Then she should have stood her ground without facing Gemma or communicating with her in any way and, eventually, Gemma would have followed. At this point Gemma could have been praised to reinforce recovery. Remember that on the day after the incident, Gemma's fear was only mild when compared to the phobic response that eventually developed. If this procedure had been carried out on each of the subsequent walks, Gemma's apprehension would have gradually diminished, and eventually she would have walked past the site without hesitation.

Curing The Problem

Gemma's fear was cured by counter conditioning her fearful association with the whistle, the sound of crowds and the footpath. The owner had a video tape of a football match that was known to elicit Gemma's anxiety. The tape was played several times a day at such low levels that Gemma displayed no fearfulness. Her total diet was fed to her by hand a piece at a time following each roar of the crowd, or occurrence of the referee's whistle. Being a Labrador, Gemma was highly motivated by food and the fact that her entire daily ration was used meant that its presence was very important to her. Once Gemma had learnt the new relationship between the sounds and the food, her owner was able to gradually increase the volume. This process took several weeks. The owner then brought a referee's whistle and blew it, quietly at first, before each piece of food.

During the next stage, feeding took place outside the home and increasingly closer to the location of the original incident. Ultimately, food was provided in the form of hand feeding by the school children, during half time, on the touch line of the pitch. The whole process took some eight weeks from start to finish. This may not have been necessary, but a prolonged and graduated counter-conditioning process is beneficial because fear must not be triggered at any time.

Flooding

Some commentators have suggested that counter-conditioning is not necessary as a means of reducing fear, and that increased exposure to whatever causes the fear without the opportunity to escape achieves the objective. A 'stick them in and let them get on with it' approach.

This theory has been tested. The results showed that animals denied the opportunity to escape display fewer attempts to escape, when eventually given the chance, than animals that always have the opportunity to move away. However this process is unpleasant for the animal, and although some do show reduced fear, others show reduced attempts to escape but no reduction in fear - and some even show an increase in fear. When an animal gets to the point where it no longer attempts to escape, despite its fear, it has reached a state of learned helplessness. The human equivalent of this state is, 'whatever I do nothing works - so what's the point in trying'. Flooding is unethical, cruel, unrealiable and unnecessary, because the kinder and more effective technique of counter-conditioning is so readily available.

Drugs

Drugs can be a useful way of supporting attempts to help a dog overcome its fear, and your vet may suggest their use. It is important that you are aware that drugs are not a substitute for behaviour modification, but make it possible for learning to take place in severe cases. Having said that, it is important to note that drug support is not necessary in the majority of cases, even difficult ones, and its use is normally short term.

Owners often feel that they have seen no benefit from drug support because they anticipated that it would make their pet sedentary. Presumably this is sometimes because of previous experience with drugs that cause sedation. These are undesirable, except as emergency treatment when the alternative is a dog being subjected to the emotional trauma of fear. The effect can make a dog look drunken, which is distressing to watch. We can only guess how the dog feels.

What is more important, drugs that sedate reduce the dog's capacity to learn that it is not frightened, and are therefore unhelpful in a treatment programme. What drug support should provide is an altered emotional state (less reaction in the arousal side of its nervous system) without causing sedation, making it possible for the owner to change the dog's behaviour (also see fireworks and thunderstorms below).

One use of drug treatments that has proved successful involves a combination of Phenobarbitone and Beta Blockers. The absence of sedation allows the dog to learn that the experience is no longer associated with the sensations that result from the activation side of our model.[1]

There is increasing interest in the use of alternative medicines as a way of reducing fear. If you feel that you would like to explore this approach, in addition to implementing the techniques to modify your dog's behaviour, you should ask your vet to refer you to a vet who specialises in this field.

Thunder And Fireworks

Unfortunately it can be difficult to treat a fear if the event that causes it is infrequent or unpredictable. This is the case with thunder and fireworks. Videos, audio tapes and sound effect compact discs can be used, but sometimes these can reproduce sounds too inaccurately to be useful. However, you can still counter-condition your dog's fear of stimuli associated with sounds (see Chapter 16). Drug support such as the combination described above can be helpful as a means of reducing or preventing fear if it is introduced prior to a firework or a thunderstorm season and maintained throughout it.

Somewhere To Hide

It is often a good idea to give the dog a den to hide in until the "danger" has passed, by using a purpose built wooden box to fit over its bed, with an aperture in one side to allow your dog an easy access or exit. This would have to be used all the time so that your dog becomes familiar with it as its den. If your dog has an indoor kennel, you can cover the top and three sides with a heavy cloth. Alternatively, you can place your dog's bed under the stairs or in a small room such as the bathroom. Don't close the door to any of these locations because your dog may panic if you do. If your dog already has a place it likes to go to when frightened, let it go there. Close all the curtains so that the room is dark and flashes cannot be seen. What may also help is playing the radio or television so loud that sounds outside the house are less obvious. When your dog eventually emerges from its hideaway, it should be praised and rewarded in the hope that this will help it recover more quickly on the next occasion.

Many dogs cannot settle in one place and keep moving in an attempt to find a better place to hide, which they never find. Others are not inclined to hide away but seek out their owners and clamber onto them, because the close proximity makes them feel more secure. If this happens to you, you must try and ignore your dog. If it climbs on you, quietly push it away. This may seem harsh thing to do when your dog needs you, but if it becomes dependent upon getting close you when it is frightened, it will have less hope of coping when you are away from home.

Shy of Strangers

Dogs that display fear aggression (see Chapter 15) towards people cause concern for their owners, and this is a problem often treated by specialists in pet behaviour. The development of fear aggresion often goes unnoticed by the pet owner, as the dog merely begins to show apprehension or shyness in the presence of strangers, which does not cause any initial concern. In many cases the start of the transformation from shyness to fear aggression occurs as the dog reaches the end of its juvenile period and matures into an adult.

The most likely cause of shyness is insufficient social contact with people during the first weeks of life. A bad experience at the hands of people is another possibility. Owners of dogs adopted at an older age, from a rescue society for example, frequently attribute any shyness to mistreatment in a previous household. Although this can be the case, a lack of early experience remains the most likely cause, particularly if the tendency to apprehension is shown in the presence of experiences other than strangers. It is therefore most important that puppies enjoy a wide range of positive experiences with a variety of people in early life. What can you do, however, to improve the situation if you already have a cautious Collie, a shy Sheltie or an apprehensive Airedale?

It is a mistake to try and cajole your dog into making friends, by pushing it forwards with words of encouragement such as "Go and say hello!" when you meet people. This would highlight the problem, resulting in your dog's tendency to avoid the individual concerned and other strangers with more determination than before.

The trick to curing people shyness lies in teaching your dog to relax in the company of strangers. This can be achieved in several ways. One of the approaches you can adopt is to stroke your dog and talk to it soothingly when it is relaxed. However this technique can be fraught with problems because mis-timing will result in you unwittingly praising your dog for being apprehensive, resulting in a tendency to display greater apprehension towards a widening range of people. It is better to avoid this possibility by encouraging a more direct, pleasant association with the people your dog encounters. How this is achieved is dependent upon whether your dog is interested in food, games with toys, or some other activity.

Using Food

It is a useful ploy to give visitors (and strangers encountered away from home) titbits to feed your dog, in order for the encounter to be regarded as pleasant, rather than frightening, for your dog. However, it is important to give the visitor enough food so that they can feed it intermittently throughout the time they are with your dog and still be in possession of some when they walk away. This will ensure that your dog's friendly interest in the person is maintained throughout the period of contact, and it will want them to come back as they walk away, because they still have some of the food. To avoid the possibility that your dog may be overfed using this method, its daily food allocation can be reduced by a percentage which is kept for use during the day.

Be sensible about the type of food you load your long-suffering vistor with: if your dog is normally fed tinned or fresh meat, some of its mixer biscuit should be used, or a pelleted complete food. It is asking a lot of a visitor to plunge his or her hand into a can of dogfood at nicely spaced intervals throughout the stay with you.

Using Toys

An alternative - or additional - approach is the use of a favourite toy of convenient size. Keep the toy where your dog can see it, but out of its reach. Whenever you come home, get up in the morning or otherwise find that yourself, family and friends are enthusiastically greeted by your dog, it should be ignored. Whoever your dog is greeting should make their way as quickly as possible to where the toy is kept, when it should be taken down and used to initiate play. At the end of each period of greeting, replace the toy and the person concerned can interact with your dog normally. Over a time your dog should become obsessed with the toy and associate it with pleasant interaction and greeting behaviour. Once this has been achieved you can use the toy to help your dog greet visitors with whom it is unfamiliar. Give the toy to the person to throw, retrieve it from your dog once it has got it and give it back to the person for them to throw again. In time your dog should be happy to cut out the middle man and take the toy straight to the person who throws it.

You can also carry the toy with you when you walk your dog and give it to people that you meet and have the opportunity to engage in conversation. They can then use the toy to invite your dog to play, which should quickly result in your dog enjoying their company rather than being anxious about it. If playing is not possible - because of traffic, for example - the fact that the person is holding the toy should help to maintain your dog's interest.

Using Body Language

Dogs are, of course, very responsive to body language, and the stance adopted by an individual can make a lot of difference to a shy dog's reaction to them. If your dog is shy in the presence of strangers, it is better to introduce it whilst the person is sitting down or squatting on their haunches, so that they appear to be less threatening. In your home it can be advantageous to introduce people when they are sitting in your main living area where your dog is used to relaxed social contact. The passive body posture of the visitor should produce a more positive response from your dog, than if its first introduction is of a looming stranger advancing over the threshold (see the next Chapter).

If your dog is very fearful, strangers should start off by avoiding eye contact and by dropping the food or toy to the floor without any attempt to communicate. Once your dog starts to solicit the food or the toy, they can gradually build up some interaction.

If your dog is not particularly motivated by titbits or toys you may have to associate the person with something else your dog does like. If, for example, a new neighbour has to be introduced to your dog, ask them to visit every day at meal times so that they can put your dog's food down for it may help where titbits failed. If it is appropriate, you can get the person concerned to take your dog for a few walks, either with you or on their own, depending on the circumstances.

The effect of all these approaches can be improved if you actively encourage people to become involved in developing your dog's confidence, rather than just using the techniques on an ad hock basis in the course of everyday events. This will also help to speed up the rate of progress. The simple rule is: the more people a dog makes friends with, the more able to cope with the new people it will become.

Four Wheel Phobia.

Does your dog dread a spin in the saloon so much that it refuses to get in? Some dogs just don't want to get into their owner's car at all, for a number of reasons. Fear of travelling is one of the obvious ones. This is not normally the result of an incident, but more commonly because of an unpleasant association with car travel, like being sick, or just a fear of the vehicle's movement due to lack of early experience. Some people have little reason to put their dog in the car because they exercise it close to home; as a result the associations the dog develops with the car can be unpleasant ones, such as trips to the vet for injections.

To overcome your dog's fear of getting into the car, you can make the process of getting in a game it enjoys. Start by opening two of the side doors so that, to your dog, the car looks like a tunnel. With your dog on a lead, climb in and don't look back. There will come a point at which the lead tightens because your dog refuses to move, but keep the tension on the lead by pulling gently and remain absolutely silent.

As a result of your efforts to get out of the other side of the car, your dog will eventually get in. When it does, continue to look in the direction you are going, but lavish it with lots of excited vocal praise. When you climb out of the car your dog will follow you. Run round to the side you got in and repeat the process, over and over again with great enthusiasm. Who needs a Jane Fonda workout?

Your dog should gradually become so excited about this new game that it will start to jump in before you. At this point you can take a break on one of the car seats, and make a fuss of it. If you have a hatch-back or estate car, put the back seat down, open the rear door and change the game to one where you get in the side of the car and out of the back and vice-versa. Rest periods are now taken in the luggage compartment!

En Route Distress

By the time you have worked off a few pounds, your dog will be happily getting in the car. This can be reinforced by feeding it all its meals in the car for the next few weeks, initially with the engine off and ultimately with it running, but don't start the engine until your dog has climbed in.

So now we have a dog that is happy about getting in the car, but how can we get it to enjoy travelling? The majority of dogs that are anxious about car travel never get to the point where they refuse to get in one. They will however, pant anxiously throughout the journey and even salivate copiously, which is a physiological response to anxiety, as, in some cases, is vomiting. If you suspect that travel sickness rather than anxiety is the cause of the vomiting, medication may be required, and you should discuss the matter with your vet.

If your dog's distress is caused by fear, the objective is to develop a pleasant association with car travel. Aim for very short journeys that end somewhere your dog enjoys: a park or the countryside for example on the outward journey, and home to a portion of its daily food. It is crucial that the journeys increase in length slowly, which mean that you may have to start by driving your car only short distances before parking it and walking the rest of the way, and vice-versa on the way home.

Dogs that will not walk:

Dogs that are too frightened to walk are often accidentally taught to keep stopping by their owners (See Gemma's story, page 197). Sometimes this fear can result in the dog being determined to dictate the direction of the walk. Whatever the case, a dog's reluctance to walk can make life very difficult.

To overcome this, use an extending lead attached to your dog's buckled (i.e. non-slip) collar. Assuming it is safe to do so, when your dog stops, release the brake on the lead and walk away from it. When you get to the end of the lead, stand with your back to your dog, avoid eye contact and resist the temptation to encourage it to move, all of which would reinforce reluctance to move. Remain in this position until your dog gets up and follows you. This process may take several minutes on the first occasion. When it moves, start walking away from your dog whilst encouraging it vocally, but don't look back. Your encouragement should increase in tempo and pitch the closer your dog gets, and when it finally reaches your side, praise it effusively while still walking.

If your dog stops before or after it reaches you, repeat the process. Your dog's inclination to stop should reduce and, if fearful, its recovery should occur more quickly on each occasion. This approach can be combined with clicker training (see Chapter 11). In this case clicker training can be used by giving a click-treat when your dog catches up with you, and intermittently while it is walking well.

Incentive Walks:

Your dog's willingness to walk can be increased if it anticipates a destination it likes. This can be to a relative or friend's house, the park or your car. For incentive walks to work you will have to repeat the route several times in succession so that your dog can build up an expectation of where it is going. It often helps if the person the dog is most fond of walks in front of whoever is holding its lead.

Willingness can also be increased if your dog is fed a meal when it arrives at a destination, or at the furthest point out on a curricular route. You can do this by carrying the food in a shoulder bag if you are going to the park or the countryside, or store the food at the location you are walking to, such as friend's house. Once your dog learns that it has to go out to eat, it will be more likely to want to face up to the big wide world to go on its 'hunting' trips. If your dog is obsessed with toys you can adopt the same approach by only playing games at the furthest point out on each walk.

Whatever methods of incentive used, it is possible to slowly increase the number and range of walks. If your dog is frightened of traffic, you must abide by the principles of counter-conditioning as much as possible. To do this ensure that you walk your dog in quiet areas or pick quiet times of day to start with. Then gradually build up the level of stimulation by going into busier areas as your dog improves.

NOTES

1.   Walker, R. 1993 Phenobarbitone and Propanolol Protocol Sheet. Association of Pet behaviour Counsellors.

Further Reading

Gray, J.A. *The Pschology of Fear and Stress* (Cambridge University Press 1987)

Gross, R.D. *Pschology - The Science of Mind and Behaviour (2nd Ed.)* (Hodder and Stoughton 1992)

Lieberman, D.A. *Learning Behaviour and Cognition (2nd Ed.)* (Brookes Cole Publishing Co. California 1993)

O'Farrell, V. *Manual of Canine Behaviour* (British Small Animal and Veterinary Association Cheltenham England 1986)

— 14. —

Territorial Aggression

In chapter 6 we saw how a dog's barking at people outside its home is often reinforced by its owner's response. But to be reinforced, the barking must have an original cause. You can normally tell what the cause is by the type of bark and the dog's general demeanour. Your dog's bark will sound very different when a member of your family is outside the door, rather than a complete stranger.

The most common reason why dogs bark at people who come near their territory is to make them go away. In most cases people do go away, which increases the dog's confidence to bark at the next potential intruder. Of course dogs do not realise that people have no intention of entering. To them it seems as if they have successfully chased them off. Significantly, the people the majority of dogs like to bark at the most are those who deliver the post or newspapers and those who take away the trash. This is because they always go away and seem to be easy targets.

Dogs can learn to discriminate between strangers by the association of certain stimuli. For example, a dog can recognise the person delivering the post, even if it can't see them, by the sound of them stopping at every house, the sound of other dogs in the area barking at them, the sound of their particular footsteps etc. The time of day can also allow the dog to anticipate their arrival. If the postman always arrives just after the family gets up, the dog will be more ready to react.

At the heart of the problem lies the fact that the pack animals from which dogs have descended have a strong sense of territory. This inheritance is compounded in a domestic situation because we put dogs in a space with defined boundaries and call it home. Through selective breeding, man has enhanced the guarding behaviour of some breeds more than others, but this drive is present in even the most affable. After companionship, one of the most popular reasons for getting a dog is its potential as a burglar deterrent. However, this usefulness can become a liability if warning barks develop into overt displays of aggression.

In most cases the risk of a visitor or passer-by being bitten is far greater than the chance that the dog will have to fight off the unwelcome intruders. It is important to remember that owners are legally liable for any injuries caused by their dogs to anyone - even a burglar! In extreme cases, magistrates can issue a destruction order against the dog, and at the time of writing they are obliged to do so if a case is successfully brought under the Dangerous Dogs Act of 1991. This is in addition to any compensation that may be awarded to the claimant.

Not many incidents have such a drastic conclusion, but you should check that you are insured against such an eventuality. Happily, with a little forethought, we can make sure that incidents do not happen. Breed variation and training aside, two types of dog are likely to display high levels of territorial behaviour:

- The fearful dog (see Chapter 15) has a vested interest in seeing visitors off.
- The dominant dog (see Chapter 12) because of its confidence within its family/pack, may take the lead in initiating territorial behaviour.

The latter may even redirect its aggression towards its owners if they frustrate it by trying to interfere. If a dog is frightened of strangers but has developed a sense of high status within the family/pack and the confidence to display territorial behaviour, its displays of aggression can be explosive.

What Can Be Done To Control The Situation?

- A high percentage of the dog population displays an acceptable level of territorial behaviour that is controlled with a quiet word from their owners
- Most dogs readily accept people into the house once their owners have let them in.

If this applies to your dog, the advice below may be unnecessary. However it is my experience that what some owners regard as being 'nothing to worry about' as far as the behaviour of their dog on the doorstep is concerned, verges on being serious, and it is important that you are sensitive to what could go wrong if something unexpected happens.

For example, you may be happy that your dog stands and barks at people until you let them in, but what happens if someone throws their hands up in the air and runs off down the garden path in fright? Can you rely on your dog not to chase them?

This may sound obvious, but you should avoid actively encouraging the development of territorial behaviour. Unaware that dogs only start to display territorial behaviour when they become adult, owners sometimes become concerned that their young dog will never woof at people that approach their home. As soon as they hear its first attempts, they are delighted and praise it profusely. This starts a process of reinforcement, which, with repetition, can generate an undesirable level of aggression. Territorial behaviour may develop to undesirable levels if a dog can see lots of people passing the home. Maybe it climbs onto a chair and looks through the window. If your dog uses a vantage point such as this, it is a good idea to deny it access to the location so as to reduce the unwanted reinforcement process.

If your dog barks when people actually approach your home but stops when it knows that you are in control of the situation, praise it.

If however, your dog is inclined to bark too much, your attempts to control it may make it more frantic, either because it seems to your dog that the whole 'pack' is barking together, or because its barking then becomes attention-seeking behaviour. In this case you should only reward your dog when it chooses not to display territorial behaviour, and ignore it when it does.

Dogs are normally conditioned to guard the threshold at the front of the home they live in because this is where they stand and bark when they hear potential intruders. If you just open the door and invite somebody in, your dog is faced with the dilemma of whether or not to back up its bravado by challenging them. It is not fair to expect it to have to discriminate between people you want it to let in, and those you want to keep outside. Unless your dog already has a really good relationship with the visitors and will recognise them as soon as you open the door, it is a good idea to remove your dog completely - perhaps to another room such as the kitchen, or further down the hall behind a childgate - before letting your visitor in. Your visitor can then be invited to sit down wherever you and your dog normally relax before you bring it into the room. Since the visitor is now:

- already in the house
- sitting down
- away from the critical location of the threshold

...your dog is more likely to be accepting.

If you are unsure about how your dog will respond to someone, you can keep it on the lead to start with, so that you have a chance to assess its attitude without putting the visitor at risk. If necessary you can follow the advice on introducing dogs that are shy of strangers in chapter 13.

Stopping Extreme Territorial Behaviour

The advice given above is more than enough for the owners of most dogs, but if your dog is extremely territorial, you can counter-condition its response to the sound of someone coming to the door (see Chapter 13 for the principles of counter-conditioning). You may have to inhibit its aggressive behaviour before you will be able to reinforce relaxed behaviour. To do this you may want to use the conditioned avoidance techniques which are discussed in chapter 5.

It is my belief that it is often better to alter excessive territorial behaviour before tackling a dog's aggression towards other people or dogs away from home. This seems especially appropriate if the aggression is motivated by fear (see Chapter 15). Opportunities to develop territorial behaviour seem to develop a dog's confidence to display aggression in other situations, regardless of whether the aggression is towards other people, dogs, or anything else. Therefore it is easier and safer to set up and control training sessions in your house, with a stooge coming to the front door, than out in the street.

Some people are worried that reducing their dog's inclination to display territorial behaviour will stop it from guarding their home, but your dog is unlikely to associate the process described below with what happens when someone is actually trying to break in. When you are at home your dog will always be allowed to woof once or twice to let you know someone is about, and when you are asleep or away from home your dog is still likely to deter intruders, but you should keep it away from vantage points where it can bark at everyone who goes by when you are out.

It is important that during the development of this learning you seek the help of volunteers to act as stooges. These can provide enough repetitions in each session to make sure that appropriate learning takes place and their repeated returns to the door will ensure that your dog continues to associate the use of the training discs described below with failure.

1. Introduce the training discs by following the instructions that come with them (see Chapter 5).

2. Use the training discs to stop chase behaviour towards an inappropriate play object such as a rolled-up pair of socks. This is so you can be sure that the technique has the desired effect of interrupting a behaviour before you start using it as a

217

means of inhibiting territorial aggression. Each time your dog chooses not to chase the item] it with praise, a titbit produced from your pocket or another reinforcer. If your dog is not interested in chasing things, try using the discs to stop it jumping up (see p 111).

3a.   Arrange for a volunteer (someone at whom your dog will be likely to bark aggressively) to knock on the door, ring the doorbell, post an old newspaper or whatever will cause your dog to rush at the door and bark. When it does, click the discs, then throw them to the ground behind your dog as it approaches the door. Do not speak to, or look at your dog, so that you do not seem to be associated with the arrival of the discs. Your volunteer should move away from the door (do not open the door) and return almost immediately: they should only walk a few paces away. In the meantime you should pick the discs up and get ready to repeat the sequence.

3b.   The process will probably have to be repeated some five or six times or more, before it occurs to your dog that every time it gets aggressive, the noise of the discs occurs and this signals its failure to chase the person away. When the penny drops, your dog should choose not to rush at the door and will avoid excessive barking, although it may still give an alarm bark. You can tell an alarm bark by the characteristic short "woofs" that tend to be very few in number. There is a big contrast between this and your dog flying at the door and giving off as many barks as it can, machine-gun fashion.

3c.   Your response to your dog's non-aggressive behaviour should be animated: you should be beaming with happiness, gushing praise and invite your dog to another part of the house, i.e. away from the point where it was being stimulated to bark, so that you can reward it by feeding a titbit, introducing a toy, praise etc.

3d.   Your volunteer should go away and return every few seconds at least six more times before the session stops. Hopefully this will provide you with six opportunities to reward non-aggressive behaviour. If your dog reverts to barking, use the discs then try again to get a minimum of six repetitions of appropriate behaviour for you to reward.

4.   Repeat the process above as often as possible, on as many different days as possible, using as many volunteers as possible, and do it at different times of the day.

5.   Once your dog responds well every time, you are ready to start using this approach in the course of every day events, such as the arrival of the postman, and whenever aggression is displayed away from home. However do not try to use the discs as a means of stopping your dog's aggressive behaviour if it is being aggressive towards you or anyone else that is holding the discs. It may be too obvious to your dog that the person using the discs is making them click and then throwing them to the ground. It may see this as a confrontational act.

Points to remember:

•   Your dog should believe that its behaviour causes the discs, so you must pretend their sounds have nothing to do with you

•   During the development stage the dog must learn to associate the sound of the discs with its failure to make your volunteers go away

•   You must properly balance out the use of these techniques with an incentive for appropriate behaviour, so that you can reinforce it. (Also see Chapter 15)

Dogs That Attack The Post

Some dogs will pull the post, or anything else pushed through the letterbox, out of the hands of the deliverer. The item is then enthusiastically shredded, or at the very least left with tooth marks. This behaviour is often seen in dogs that display a high level of territorial aggression, and it seems to be a way in which the dog vents its frustration at not being able to get at the person delivering.

In some dogs, the characteristics of their breed has complicated this behaviour. Terriers, for example, can be so stimulated by the appearance of their 'prey' that they won't stop short of total destruction! Further complications can arise if the dog then guards its trophy, or becomes defensive because it anticipates its owner's annoyance and punishment for damaging the post.

If you experience this problem, the short-term solution to protecting your post - and the delivery person's fingers - is to attach a post-box on the inside of the door to catch the post and prevent the dog from getting at it. In some severe cases the dog will pull the box off the door, so a waterproof box will have to be put on the outside wall instead.

- In most cases, the problem itself should be treated as an expression of territorial aggression, especially if the dog is also attacking the deliverer of the post.
- If your dog is only interested in what comes through the letterbox, try the techniques described in chapter 8 for stopping chase and predatory behaviour.
- If your dog treats the captured post as a trophy it does not want you to have, you will need to reduce its sense of status.(See Chapter 12)
- As with all behaviour problems, consider how much of the

problem may be attention-seeking. It may be useful to treat this stealing of the post as you would treat the stealing and guarding of any inappropriate item. (See Chapter 6)

- Try making the post unattractive to your dog, by getting neighbours to deliver envelopes stuffed with chilli peppers. If an unpleasant association has been made, sprinkling chilli powder inside the letterbox will ensure that all the letters will have the same scent, and your dog will leave well alone.

Making a meal of it.

Food is an important resource for us all. This may seem an obvious statement, but in the western world with its easily available abundance of food, its importance can seem less evident. Few people have to make any more effort than pushing a shopping trolley around the local supermarket. You need do no more to defend your purchases than place a "next customer" sign on the checkout conveyer belt to declare that the goods are yours. Our experience of food is very different from that of our prehistoric hunting-gathering ancestors.

In much the same way, the situation of the domestic dog bears little relation to its ancestor, the wolf. The average family dog no longer has to roam the wilderness in search of prey. There are few complications associated with the standard tin of dog food. The family dog lives in the lap of luxury, its meals are provided regularly by the generous human members of the pack. As a consequence the domestic dog expends very little energy obtaining its food, so you would think its need to defend it would no longer exist. This, of course, is not the case, because the dog's instinctive drive to protect the resource of food remains very strong. Consequently, aggression over food is a problem encountered by a considerable number of owners.

The aggression is not necessarily a full blown, teeth bared, lip curled attack. More often than not it is limited to a warning growl at someone who has got too close. Nonetheless it is an expression of aggression which indicates the dog is unhappy with the situation. It is often assumed that a dog which displays aggression over food is a dominant individual, but not all dogs that are hostile over food are dominant. Even low-ranking members of the group may display resistance if they feel their meal is coveted by another.

Defence Mechanism

Defence of food is an instinctive behaviour and steps should be taken to prevent or cure it. It has long been advocated that the best course of action is to "show the dog who's boss", and ensure it knows its owner can take its food away. This point of view is, I think, mistaken. The correct way to prevent or cure a dog's aggression over food is to remove its need to guard it.

This point is illustrated by one of the worst cases I have ever seen. Some clients consulted me about a Golden Retriever which had a habit of growling over its food. A local dog trainer advised them to "show the dog who's boss" and take its food away when it was eating. They were also instructed to smack the dog on the nose if it growled at them. These actions convinced the dog that its food was under threat. This led to an increase in its displays of aggression if the owners came into the vicinity of the dog when it was eating, because it anticipated confrontation. The final straw came when the male owner put the food down; the dog pinned him against the wall. Leaving the food, it stood with its front paws on the husband's chest and snarled in his face. It was a frightening episode, but not as frightening as the archaic advice the owners had originally received.

Oblique Angle

In most cases, all that is required to prevent or cure the problem is a bit of lateral thinking, some time, and a willingness to abandon gun-boat diplomacy. It should be obvious that if a dog guards its food through a fear that it may be taken away, removing the threat should remove the problem.

If your dog shows an intention to try and bite when it is in possession of its food, do not attempt to use the method described below without first ensuring your safety, and the safety of those around you. You may be able to do this by asking a responsible adult member of your family to stand behind your dog and hold it on a lead. This will prevent it from having the opportunity to snap at the person feeding it if it misinterprets their intentions. If you are on your own, or you think that you have to be more cautious, you can tether your dog before you start so that it cannot reach you. If you are unsure about the advisability of proceeding, or think that it is too dangerous, seek further help (see p 281). If your dog growls at any time during these routines, end the session and put the food you have in your possession away and start again later, but revert to an earlier stage.

Start with two feeding bowls, one empty and the other full. Put the empty bowl on the ground in front of your dog and hold the full one in your hand out of its reach.

Sit on a chair on the opposite side of the empty food bowl to your dog. Take a handful of food from the full bowl and hold it in the air above your dog's head. Eventually, your dog will sit because it is looking up at the food. When it does, move your arm down as if to put the food in the bowl. If your dog moves to take the food, lift your hand again, but don't say anything. Soon your dog will realise that the way to get the food to go into the empty bowl is to sit and wait for it to be put in. The absence of commands will remove any semblance

223

of confrontation, and from your dog's point of view it will be apparent that there is no point growling at you because it wants you to stay. When your dog finally learns to wait, you can release the food into the bowl, saying "take it".

When your dog has finished the small amount of food in the bowl, repeat the process and continue in this manner until all the food has gone. Put the bowl you were using where your dog cannot get to it, without letting it see that you have run out of food.

After hand-feeding in this manner every mealtime, your presence will become a positive force instead of a negative one. When you think this has happened, dispense with the chair and take a step away from the feed bowl between handfuls. This should result in your dog learning to associate your approach with the pleasant event of the arrival of food.

In time, you can move further away between handfuls and give your dog larger portions each time you return. Ultimately your dog should receive more food than it can eat before you return with the next portion. To maintain your dog's interest in the food that you wish to give it, make the food you are returning with more palatable than the food it has got. If your dog prefers wet food to dry, all the food it is given in its bowl should be dried biscuit, and the food you return to feed it with should be tinned meat.

Eventually you should be able to feed your dog all but a few handfuls of its food at the beginning of each meal, and return with tastier morsels which it receives if it sits back and lets you put them into the bowl.

The owners of the problem Golden Retriever managed to cure its aggression and everything was fine for two years. One day however, the dog growled as the husband passed his feed bowl. The growl turned into an attempted bite as the husband hit out, and the dog was put to sleep. If only they had gone back to the advice I had given them, the dog would not have bitten and would still be alive.

Effective Methods

The lesson for the rest of us is that this technique does work. When your dog stops growling, you can carry on adding food to its bowl to reinforce the training, reminding it that your presence is a good thing.

In some cases, changing what you feed a dog that has developed a tendency to guard its food may make a difference. Dogs are more inclined to defend tastier foods, so it is often a good idea to change the diet gradually to something the dog is not so keen on. It is difficult to make recommendations about diet as individual dogs' preferences vary a little, so trial and error may be necessary.

Free And Easy

Adopting a free-feeding method can also help to combat this type of aggression. The system favours dried foods which can be left out and to which the dog can help itself. If the bowl is kept topped up and water is constantly available, most dogs will eventually regulate their own intake.

Unfortunately, this method is not conducive to the development of regular toileting routines, which can be established more easily if the dog's feeding times are pre-determined. If the system works, the dog's inclination to guard its food should decrease as the abundance of food reduces its value.

—— 15. ——

Fear Aggression

All aggression involves an element of fear, even that displayed by confident dogs in rank-related disputes. What we are concentrating on here, however, is quite specific. Generally, a dog will move away from something it is frightened of. But when it can't, it has two choices: grin and bear it, or make the threat go away. It can do this by showing aggression. Since the dog is in a state of fear at the time, this is known as fear aggression.

Normally a dog's tendency to display aggression develops over time. For example, if a fearful dog is off the lead, it may avoid the other dogs it encounters; or, safe in the knowledge that it can run away if it has to, it may interact with them. However, when the dog is on a lead it cannot run away and it may attempt to make the other dog go away by growling or barking at it. In all probability the other dog will go away of its own volition or will be taken away by its owner; or the fearful dog's owner will remove it from the scene. From the dog's perspective it will seem that its display of aggression worked as a means of getting rid of the other dog, and its aggressive behaviour will be reinforced in much the same way as territorial behaviour is reinforced, by apparent success. (see Chapter 14).

The more often this scenario is repeated, the more likely the dog is to choose to display aggression in the presence of other dogs, and the more confident and overt its displays are likely to be. In severe cases, what starts as relatively quiet growling or barking develops into a very noisy display with a tendency for the dog to lunge towards what it is trying to get rid of when it is on the lead. This apparent confidence can result in people misinterpreting the true motive for the behaviour.

Some dogs become so confident in the efficacy of their displays of aggresion that they will run and attack what they are frightened of even when they are off the lead, because attack seems demonstrably the best form of defence. Failure to get a result through aggression explains why, after an initial attempt to deter them, some dogs accept the presence of visitors in their owner's home but maintain a safe distance. When the visitor prepares to leave, the dog can become unexpectedly aggressive and may try to bite them. This is because the dog knows from experience that its attempts to make the threat go away will now be successful.

This pattern of behaviour can also happen away from home when an owner stands and talks to someone. The dog may sit quietly until the person tries to move away, at which point it may lunge at them.

Aggression caused by fear is often said to be unpredictable. However, it is predictable if you know the formula. To help you visualise this, imagine that around a frightened dog there are three circles.

1. The outer circle represents the flight distance. This is the distance at which the dog might choose to move away from something it is frightened of.

2. The middle circle represents the critical distance. This is distance at which, if it is unable to flee, the dog may show aggression to make what it is frightened of go away.

3. The smallest, innermost circle is the intimate distance. This is the distance at which the dog will decide whether or not it will allow physical contact with anything that has come inside the critical distance.

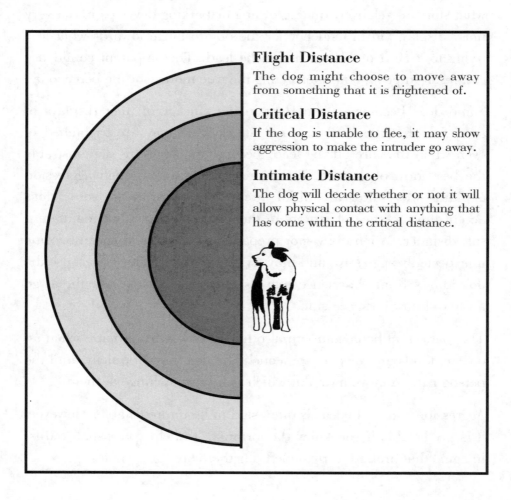

Flight Distance
The dog might choose to move away from something that it is frightened of.

Critical Distance
If the dog is unable to flee, it may show aggression to make the intruder go away.

Intimate Distance
The dog will decide whether or not it will allow physical contact with anything that has come within the critical distance.

The size of the circles will change according to the dog's sensitivity to the stimulus.

Say a dog is unsocialised with children but then becomes accustomed to them; its sensitivity will reduce and the circles will get smaller. On the other hand, if a dog that has been confident with other dogs is bitten by one, then the size of the circles, in the presence of other dogs, may be larger in future.

What the dog will react towards can be specific or generalised. For example, if it is bitten on the nose by a Jack Russell Terrier, a dog may continue to be friendly towards all other dogs except Jack Russell Terriers and dogs that look like them. In time this defensive behaviour may generalise to include dogs that look less like Jack Russells, and ultimately perhaps to dogs of all descriptions.

Similarly a dog's fear aggression towards people of one type, such as children or men, can become generalised to include people of all types.

The size of the circles around the frightened dog is also affected by the amount of stimulation caused by whatever is frightening it. Another dog lying out in the midday sun is unlikely to seem like a threat, and the size of the fearful dog's circles will be small. But if the other dog is barking at, or running near or towards the fearful dog, the circles will be larger. In a similar manner a dog may adjust to the presence of a visitor sitting in its owner's living room because they do not seem to pose a threat. If the visitor sneezes violently or stands up, the increased stimulation may cause the circles to increase in size and the dog may react defensively.

A fearful dog tends to be less reactive to strangers who ignore them than to those who try to "make friends". Many owners encourage people to ignore their dog and to "let him come round in his own time". What the owners are really doing is asking people to reduce the level of stimulation until the dog has learnt that they are not a threat and becomes desensitised to their presence. Whether or not a dog that has accepted someone's presence inside its critical distance will let them inside its intimate distance and allow them to stroke it is another matter. It may suddenly snap at someone who tries to touch it even though it has not tried, or has stopped trying, to make them maintain a critical distance.

Owner Reinforcement

Owners sometimes attempt to cure fear aggression when their dog is on the lead with harsh corrections using a check-chain and bellowed commands such as "leave it!". This can make matters worse because the dog learns to associate the presence of what it is frightened of with being hurt by its own lead. This can result in the dog becoming even more determined to make the threat go away. Although a quiet word can do the trick an owner's attempts to control his or her dog verbally may be interpreted by the dog as the owner's response to the threat, and it may redouble its efforts. Alternatively, the dog may find its owner's response rewarding and this will reinforce the behaviour.

Tightening the lead to achieve a higher level of control invariably causes the dog to tense and get ready to react, especially if the sensation has become associated with aggressive behaviour. If your dog finds something frightening and becomes aggressive towards it, you should remain relaxed and keep the lead slack. Attempts to pre-empt aggression and control the dog by saying "*Leave it... Leave it*" can work; but some dogs react as though you had said "*There's one! There's one!*". Whether this method will succeed or fail is dependent upon the nature of the dog, its previous history and the severity of the problem. If it is consistently failing there is no point in persisting with it; and in all cases the 'off' approach is preferable (See Chapter 6).

Controlling a dog that is aggressive whilst remaining relaxed yourself can be difficult to achieve. The use of a head collar such as a Halti or Gentle Leader often helps because it improves the power to weight ratio in the owner's favour. A head collar also reduces the dog's opportunity to bite by allowing the owner to turn the dog's head away from its intended target. Breaking the dog's eye contact in this way is also helpful.

The effectiveness of a head collar can be greatly improved if it is combined with a double-ended lead. This is a lead with two clips, one at each end. In normal use these leads make it possible to make the lead long or short by attaching one of the clips to one of two rings along the lead's length. However, by clipping one clip onto your dog's head collar and the other end to its ordinary collar, you will have the option of taking the lead in two hands, one controlling your dog's head, the other controlling its neck.

This will make it much more difficult for your dog to:

* lunge at someone or something.
* spin around, as some dogs do when their aggression is frustrated.
* pull backwards and slip off the headcollar.

If a difficult situation arises, it will also be much easier to put yourself between your dog and whatever is at risk.

In addition to keeping a relaxed lead, you must ensure that you do not convey any anxiety through your actions. Try to maintain a body posture indicating that you are calm, confident and relaxed when you are in situations that may cause your dog to be frightened and aggressive. This will predispose it to remain relaxed as well.

Muzzles

Ensuring the safety of other people and animals is essential and you can achieve this by using a muzzle. Many owners fear that the use of muzzle will make their dog's tendency to aggression worse. This can be the case if a muzzle is only associated with situations that make the dog fearfully aggressive; but getting a dog used to wearing a muzzle in situations that are not stressful can prevent this.

Introducing the muzzle should be done gradually so that your dog learns to accept it. Try placing the muzzle next to your dog's food bowl during feeding. Subsequently the muzzle can be put on for a few moments every so often when you are relaxing. Start by slipping it on your dog's nose and slipping it off again, without doing it up, and associate this action with lots of affection and praise. When you think your dog is getting used to it, you can fasten the muzzle for short periods of time, the duration of which can be gradually increased. Continue to praise your dog whilst it accepts the muzzle but ignore it if it tries to get it off.

If your dog continues to try to remove the muzzle, despite a gradual introduction, and proves to be good at it, you can overcome the problem by putting a non-slip (i.e. buckled) collar on your dog first and passing the strap of the muzzle under this before fastening it.

Once your dog will wear a muzzle, you can use it in any situation in which it is expedient to do so: when your dog needs veterinary examination, or when people who trigger your dog's fear aggression visit your home, or in the presence of vulnerable individuals, such as children or the elderly or frail.

Curing the problem of Fear Aggression

In many case it is possible to reduce or cure a dog's inclination to show fear aggression to people using the techniques suggested for dogs that are simply fearful (Shy of Strangers - see Chapter.13), although it is important that no-one is put at risk. You may need to keep your dog on a lead. In extreme cases it may be necessary to concentrate on stopping the dog's displays of aggression before you try to give it a more positive association with the things it is frightened of. Sometimes the best that can be hoped for is stopping the dog from being overtly aggressive, and having a group of friends that the dog learns to like, rather than the dog becoming everybody's and everything's best buddy.

One way of reducing the level of aggression displayed is to use conditioned avoidance learning (see page 108). When possible, it is better to start modifying aggressive behaviour as discussed in chapter 5.

If you have been able to modify your dog's aggressive behaviour in territorial situations and its improved behaviour can now be guaranteed, you can start to use the techniques outlined below in training sessions away from the home environment. It is a good idea to ask for volunteers to act as stooges. These can provide enough repetitions in each session to allow the association to continue between the sound of the discs, and failure. Stooges should present themselves in whatever form will trigger your dog's fearful aggression: strangers, people with dogs, cyclists, etc.

A client of mine was able to modify her dog's aggression towards other dogs, motor bikes and small vans by getting volunteers to help her, but was not able to cure her dog's aggression towards local buses because, not surprisingly, she did not know anyone who owned one. So she took the dog and stood near the bus station, where she had all the opportunity she needed to teach her dog that barking at buses would not make them go away. In this way she was able to reinforce more appropriate behaviour.

Where it is possible to arrange for help from volunteers they should be asked to move backwards and forwards at a distance from you; or to stay still whilst you repeatedly walk past them. Initially the distance between you should be such that your dog's aggression is stimulated as little as possible. For example, if your dog is fearfully aggressive towards dogs, the volunteer should walk with a dog on a lead, at some distance from you. Their dog should be of even temperament and unlikely to bark at your dog or do anything else that may unnecessarily stimulate your dog into showing aggression. If your dog, which of course will also be on a lead, displays aggression, then you should click the discs and throw them to the ground behind it. Repeat this each time your dog shows aggression to the volunteer and their dog.

When your dog chooses not to show aggression, praise it and produce food or another reinforcer (see page 98), from your pocket. The session should continue until your dog chooses to avoid showing aggression each time the dog and person pass you or you pass them.

Do not reduce the distance between yourself and the stooge to the point where it is beyond your dog's capacity to cope. Of course you must never allow the volunteer or their dog, if there is one, to be put at risk of being bitten. Remember that this exercise is only designed to stop your dog from thinking that it can make something go away. It will not make it want to be friends.

Once you no longer need to encumber yourself with the discs you can keep them in your pocket and use a clicker in your free hand to reinforce relaxation (see Chapter 11). Whether you use this method of reinforcement or another, rewards should initially be given every time appropriate behaviour is performed. Once your dog starts to look for them rather than show aggression, they should only be given when the best responses are performed, and finally given intermittently so as to continually improve your dogs behaviour.

You will need to repeat these sessions with as many stooges as possible to help generalise the learning. This can take some arranging if it involves other dogs; but you may be able to ask some of the people at a dog training club to help you - although you should not repeat the training sessions in the environment of the club. One of the associates in my practice runs special rehabilitation classes so that dogs that have fear aggression problems do not have to mix with dogs that do not, so there is an opportunity to address this problem specifically. It is to be hoped that one day this sort of approach will become commonplace.

When you feel that your dog is ready, you can start to alternate between sessions with stooges and everyday events. As before, you should be ready to use the techniques necessary to stop your dog from being aggressive and to reinforce appropriate behaviour when it occurs.

If your dog's problem involves other dogs, try to move it to the left or the right whenever other dogs are encountered so that its line of travel curves away from and around the dog. This is important, because unfamiliar dogs find direct (head to head) approaches very threatening and it is more natural for them to peel away to the left or right, giving each other the opportunity to view their body language.

Giving your dog something to do that is incompatible with aggression can be useful as a means of reducing its inclination to show it. To achieve this, teach your dog to sit or lie down as soon as you give the signal. Once you have established this you can give the signal when you encounter the stimulus towards which your dog is inclined to show fear aggression. When your dog sits or lies down, and only while it continues in this position, reward it and continue to reward it using one of the reinforcement techniques, until the stimulus has gone away. The benefit of this approach is that your dog does not have to work out what to do when it sees whatever it is frightened of. You are not telling your dog to leave the other dog alone, you are giving it something else to do, in much the same way as the 'off' technique.

Getting Back Into The Society Of Other Dogs

Once your dog has stopped showing fear aggression towards other dogs, you can start to re-integrate it by walking it with well-behaved dogs belonging to other people. Keep the dogs on their leads and wherever possible walk parallel to the other person but far enough apart to prevent your dog being able to attack the other dog if its aggression is stimulated for any reason. So long as your dog remains relaxed, reinforce its behaviour every now and then. After several successful walks, first on a lead, and then on an extending lead, you may be able to let the dogs interact without restraint. However, during this stage you should ensure the safety of the other dog by using a muzzle if necessary (see page 232).

The more your dog is walked in the company of well adjusted dogs, the more it will become accustomed to dogs in general and desensitised to their presence.

Getting Back Into The Society Of People

If your dog acts defensively towards strangers, you need to use counter-conditioning. Of course, you cannot do this if you think people may be put at risk.

In many cases the approach suggested for dogs that are shy of strangers should be sufficient (see Chapter 13); but if the problem is severe, a more systematic approach may be called for. This may be especially necessary if you have to introduce your dog to particular people such as new friends.

Start by asking individuals with whom your dog is well acquainted and friendly, to call at your house for the sole purpose of feeding it. Once the individual has entered, ask them to sit in the living room, or other area where social contact with your dog normally takes place. Bring your dog through to them on a lead attached to a non-slip (buckled) collar, and keep hold of it. Provide the person with your dog's food in a bowl. The bowl should contain all of your dog's daily ration of food, except for the titbits used in other behaviour modification and training exercises. (If the procedure can be repeated more than once each day your dog's food should be divided into the appropriate amounts.)

The visitor should feed your dog on a piecemeal basis, i.e. little and often, throughout the duration of their stay. When they get up to leave they should keep hold of some of the food so that your dog's interest in them continues.

If you start by using people your dog knows, you will familiarise it with the procedure so that it can anticipate what will happen when you involve people with whom it is less familiar. By ensuring that this is the only way in which your dog gets to eat, it should not take long for it to anticipate that visitors to your home will feed it.

Once this position is reached you can gradually substitute less familiar visitors for the familiar ones. These people should ensure that they do not make your dog feel threatened by avoiding eye contact, and, if necessary, they should start by simply dropping pieces of food on the floor or into a second bowl.

The style of interaction between the feeder and dog can gradually normalise as your dog starts to show an inclination to solicit feeding. However, until that point, the visitor must remain entirely passive. To ensure the safety of your visitors you will have to continue to hold your dog on a lead.

Freer interaction away from where feeding is taking place should only be considered if your dog is muzzled, until you are absolutely convinced that the person is not at risk. As your dog's confidence increases, gradually subsitute new, unknown visitors for those people your dog has already met.

If the counter-conditioning with strangers works well within the home, you can start to introduce the process in locations away from it. Initially you should revert to using people with whom your dog is familiar, and then less familiar, and so on. This is important because the novelty of the different environments may cause your dog to be more sensitive, and therefore more likely to react defensively in the presence of the feeder. The greater the number of locations used and the greater the variety of individuals involved, the more generalised your dog's acceptance of other people should become.

Pain-induced Aggression

Fear aggression can also result from an injury or some other source of pain, such as an ear infection. The dog's defensive behaviour can continue long after the pain has been alleviated. Once the treatment for the physical condition is complete, the dog's defensive behaviour can be counter-conditioned.

To achieve this, lightly touch your dog near the area where it has experienced pain, being careful not to trigger a fearful response. Follow this with a titbit from your hand. Over a period of time, possibly several days, you should repeat the procedure many times. Once it is clear that your dog expects the titbit when you touch it, you can gradually move closer to the site of the original pain, until your dog will no longer flinch.

—— 16. ——

Separation Problems

Does your dog bark or howl, have 'accidents' in the house, or chew up your door frames when you go to work? Do you think that when it shreds the furniture it is getting you back for leaving it all alone? Think again. It may be that your dog is undergoing a severe psychological trauma, but the question is, which one?

The problems that can occur during an owner's absence include[1]:

- over-activity
- destructiveness
- inappropriate defecation or urination in dogs that are house trained
- excessive barking

In more severe cases stereotypic behaviours (see page 116) may occur, as may vomiting and salivation. It has also been suggested that aggression directed at the owner when they try to leave can be symptomatic of an emotional state related to a separation problem.[2] In my experience this tends to be more likely in dogs that have also developed a sense of high status within their family/pack.

It is not uncommon for combinations of symptoms to occur.

Other generalised symptoms to look out for are:

- increased or decreased appetite
- increased thirst
- insomnia and restlessness

The range of possible causes for the symptoms of separation problems includes[3]:

- fear
- over-attachment to the owner (separation anxiety)
- displacement behaviour, such as a dog, frustrated by its inability to reach the people it barks at outside the house, redirecting its aggression onto the things around it
- a continuance of attention-seeking behaviours, such as barking, that the dog has learnt to perform when the owners are at home
- learned behaviour as a result of boredom, where the conse-quences of what the dog does are self-reinforcing, such as the

240

entertaining effect of feathers flying out of a pillow, or the gratifying sound of material tearing

Contrary to popular opinion the list of possible causes does not include dogs getting revenge on their owners for leaving them alone. Dogs are not capable of forming this abstract concept.

Determining why problems do occur can be difficult, because the symptoms resulting from one cause can appear to be very similar to those arising from another. However, closer inspection will allow you to make some sense of what is going on and gain an understanding of how to cure the problem.

A comparison between the two most common separation problems, fear and over-attachment to the owner (separation anxiety), will help to illustrate the point.

The Problems

Fear

As we have seen in chapter 13, it is not unreasonable for a dog to be afraid of some things such as thunderstorms or fireworks. After it has experienced a storm or fireworks, a dog may be frightened that they will recur, and it may rely on its owner's presence to provide it with a sense of security. When the owners go out, this security is removed and the dog may become distressed. This is particularly likely to be the case if thunderstorms or fireworks have occurred when the dog has been left unattended on previous occasions, and even more likely if thunderstorms or fireworks actually occur. In some cases the dog may cope with being left, unless panic is triggered by things associated with the actual experience such as the sound of the wind blowing around the house, or rain beating on the window panes in the case of thunderstorms.

Over-Attachment

The problem of over- or hyper-attachment is often compared to the human condition of separation anxiety, when apprehension arises due to the removal of significant persons or familiar surroundings.[4]

One theory suggests that the dog is seeking a surrogate mother, and will fix on one person even if there are several people living in the home. This undoubtedly occurs. But the problem often starts in later life, after the dog has spent years not being over-attached. Some dogs do not display the symptoms until their faculties start to fail them.

A typical example is a dog whose owner is at home more than usual; possibly because of a period of illness, pregnancy, extended holiday or redundancy. A period of nursing care can have the same effect, although this may also have something to do with the stress of the illness or accident, making it more likely that a dog will become dependent upon the carer. Some dogs only start to display separation problems after a family holiday because they cannot cope when everyone goes back to work and school.

Perhaps the problem is related to the tendency to form attachments to other 'pack' members, and substitute parental attachment is part of a range of attachments a dog can make with other members of the family/pack.

There is evidence to suggest that a predisposition to develop separation anxiety can be inherited.[5] However, as with all behaviour, the likelihood of the condition actually occurring will be determined by a combination of genetics and environment.[6]

It has been suggested by various authorities that there is a higher than average incidence of separation problems in dogs re-homed by rescue societies.[7] Some owners feel terribly disappointed when this happens, and comments like: 'So this is how he repays us!' are common. The above-average incidence has been attributed to the unsettling experiences the dog has gone through, but it is possible that it is sometimes due to the owners trying too hard to compensate the dog for the hard time it is thought to have had, so that it bonds excessively. The figures will also be affected by the fact that a percentage of dogs going into rescue societies do so because of existing separation problems.

How Can You Tell What The Problem Is?[8]

If your dog is frightened you are likely to see evidence of it. For example, if it is frightened of thunderstorms or fireworks when you are at home it follows that it will be frightened by them during your absence. You are likely to find that your dog likes to follow you about the house, although it may be content to lie where it can keep you in view. When you move from one room to another your dog may not immediately follow you, but remain lying where it is for a while before checking to see where you are. You may also find that it will not be distressed if it is shut in another room when you are at home, as long as whatever is frightening it is not actually occuring.

This contrasts with the behaviour you will see if your dog is over-attached to you. If this is the case, you will find that your dog needs to shadow your every move. As soon as you settle, your dog will want to sit in physical contact with you, or at least near you. If a door is shut denying your dog access to you when you are at home, it is likely to become distressed and start to whine or bark to call you back, or to scratch at the door in an attempt to follow.

If your dog is attached to one person, this behaviour will be directed at them and it will be distressed even when another person is with it. Owners of over-attached dogs often report that they cannot even go to the bathroom without their pet attempting to follow them to sit at their feet. Dogs that suffer from over-attachment are also likely to show signs of anxiety or depressed behaviour when their owners prepare to leave. When they return the dog is likely to display greeting behaviour so excessive that the dog seems relieved to see them rather that just pleased.

The distinction between the symptoms of fear and separation anxiety can be less clear. If a frightened dog is highly anxious it may behave more like dogs that are over-attached. This seems to be particularly likely if, when the dog is frightened, it is inclined rather to seek comfort from its owners than to hide. Conversely, dogs that have separation anxiety may not seem overly-attached to their owners when they are at home if their anxiety has not been reinforced very much, eg. if the owner only leaves them once or twice a year.

In fact the inter-relationship between the two conditions is not well understood.

Clues associated with your absence

A clue that can help to determine the motivation for destructive behaviour is its location. If the problem is caused by fear, the dog is simply trying to escape and destruction can occur at any door that leads to somewhere it will feel safe. Significantly, such a dog may not be destructive if it is left in a room or a house it does not associate with events that cause it to be fearful. When it does occur, destructive behaviour can be the result of an attempt to escape from the house or to get somewhere the dog considers to be safe inside, such as the owner's bedroom. The latter may occur if the dog knows that the thing of which it is frightened is outside. The dog may also dig as if to create a den to take shelter in. It may do this by digging into the corners of rooms, digging into the seat of a chair or sofa, digging into the owner's mattresses; or it may even try to get into cupboards.

Dogs that suffer from this condition may also chew things impregnated with their owner's scent. It is thought that the more the debris is disturbed the greater area of invisible barrier of the owner's scent there is for the dog to lie in, or behind, which makes it feel secure. A dog will not plan this of course, but it can learn it through experience (See Operant Learning, page 91).

Some dogs are destructive in an attempt to escape from something they are frightened of within the house rather than outside it. This can be something innocuous such as the mere presence of the vacuum cleaner or even the sound of the refrigerator switching on and off.

A client of mine noticed that her dog started to avoid the end of the kitchen where her tumble-drier stood. The tumble-drier had not previously caused a problem and when she was at home her dog's avoidance behaviour was so mild she thought nothing of it. What became problematical was the dog's habit of breaking though a door to escape from the kitchen and into the next room when left alone. In time the dog was not content to just escape from the kitchen and it continued to break through two more doors until it could gain access to the owner's bedroom where it would lie until she came home. The cause? There were mice nesting in the tumble-drier vent and the dog, a very big German Shepherd, was scared of the noise!

When the problem is caused by separation anxiety, destruction is likely to occur specifically at the door or window that would give the dog access to the route by which the owner left. The destruction can include the carpet, woodwork and plaster around the access point. As with dogs that are frightened during their owner's absence, dogs that are hyper-attached are sometimes attracted to items impregnated with their owners scent, but they tend to lie on them rather destroy them.

Barking and Howling

Dog owners sometimes fall foul of their neighbours and the local Environmental Health Department because their dogs bark or howl incessantly when left alone. Such dogs are often attempting to call their owners back home again, and because they eventually come back, the barking seems to be effective - so the dog barks with even more determination the next time it is left alone.

In the wild, one of the reasons why adult wolves howl is as a means of relocating the pack. As immature versions of their cousins, dogs generally have a greater tendency to bark more than to howl. If your dog is vocal when it is left, it is a good idea to tape it either with a long-playing cassette or a voice-activated dictaphone. (If you have the facilities, video taping is the best diagnostic tool whatever the symptoms the dog is displaying when left unattended). This will enable you to determine what sort of barking your dog is doing. This is important because there is no point in trying to treat your dog for separation anxiety, where the vocal behaviour is likely to be constant, when it is clear from the type of bark and its infrequency that it is barking at people that walk past your home.

You may be able to tell if the barking or howling is attention-seeking, because the dog will pause to listen for a response between short sessions of barking, i.e. the bit where you say 'shut up' or bang on the floor when you are at home.

Dogs that are frightened are unlikely to be vocal because they do not want to draw attention to themselves.

Loss Of Toilet Control

This can be a consequence of either fear or separation anxiety and is a result of the activation side of our model of the nervous system.

Different Approaches To Prevent Two Problems:

1.   Fear

Preventing the development of separation problems caused by fear is related to habituation and socialisation (see Chapters 2 and 3).

2.   Separation anxiety

Ensuring that very young puppies are not over-bonded to their owners should help to prevent over-dependence.[9] It is important that a puppy is accustomed to periods of time when it is separated from its owners, the duration of these separations being gradually increased (see indoor kennel page 44).

Most vocal, destructive and toileting behaviour caused by separation anxiety occurs within half an hour of the owner's departure[10] because the dog is in a state of anxiety at the time its owner leaves. You can reduce the effect of the signs which enable your dog to predict your departure. The emotional response to sounds such as car keys, and sights such as you putting your shoes on can be latently habituated (see p 88) in puppies by associating them with your presence.[11] For example, you can repeatedly put on outdoor clothing and rattle your car keys without going out. You can progress to going out of the house and returning after a few seconds. The period of time outside the house can be gradually increased and stimuli such as starting and turning off the car engine can be introduced before re-entering the home.

It is possible to continue doing all those things that are not recommended for dog owners to do (see under Controlling Separation Anxiety later in this chapter) and nothing untoward will happen. However, instances of owners acting inappropriately seem to be present when the problem occurs because a dog that is predisposed to develop separation anxiety is given an environment in which that anxiety is reinforced. It makes sense to reduce the chance of disaster by not providing the environment for over-attachment to develop. Most people are unable to anticipate whether their dog will develop separation anxiety, so all owners should follow the essence of the approach discussed below in *'controlling separation anxiety'*. If this prevents the unnecessary euthanasia or rehoming of some of the dogs that have the potential to develop the problem, taking the preventative medicine is worth it.

However, if you feel you can determine whether the problem is developing or not, go ahead and live with your dog in the way you want to, but be prepared to alter your approach if you think your dog is starting to get too clingy. You never know when your dog might have to cope without you.

Curing Separation Problems

Fear

The way to cure a separation problem caused by fear is to cure the fear. This is a procedure that involves changing the dog's response to the things that distress it (see Chapter 13). For example, if it is frightened of strangers and it is fearful that strangers may come to the home while you are out, you will have to change its response to strangers (see Shy of Strangers page 204).

The German Shepherd's fear of the tumble-drier, described above, was counter-conditioned, after the removal of the mice, by placing a food bowl containing its meal in the tumble-drier some time before feeding every day. When it was the dog's meal time the food came from the tumble-drier.

Fear of thunder storms and fireworks may require counter-conditioning (see page **196**) using recordings of those sounds. These will only be effective if:

1. the recording is good enough

2. your sound system is up to it

3. your dog is convinced.

Your dog may have been conditioned to respond fearfully to a stimulus because of its association with the event that frightens it. For example, you may have to counter-condition your dog's response to the sound of heavy rain because it has learnt that thunderstorms may follow. Recreating this sound can be achieved by using a garden hose positioned so that it will spray a window or conservatory roof.

I once had to treat a Dobermann that tried to dig holes in the corners of its owner's living room because it was fearful of the sound of the water pipes making a "clunk" noise when the person who lived in the flat above turned off his tap. The dog had also become reactive to the sound of any water going through any of the pipes because it anticipated that the "clunk" might follow. In addition to counter-conditioning his fear by using tapes and the live sound of water running through the pipes, we were able to help by giving him a dog flap so that he could go into the garden and did not feel trapped when these noises occurred. Once he had more control over his ability to get away, the dog was able to cope with the sounds much better.

Controlling Separation Anxiety

Much of the treatment for problems caused by over-attachment involves altering the contrast between the owner's presence and their absence.

These techniques will help to do this. As with other areas of this book the extent to which you will need to implement the advice will be governed by what you think is necessary.

If your dog is very dependent upon you and therefore likely to become more anxious if you change your relationship too quickly, introduce these techniques in sequence. Move from one stage to the next when your dog seems to be coping without signs of stress.

1.   Affection

An important way in which you can influence your dog's behaviour is by ensuring that you give it attention when it is relaxed about being with you. You can ensure this is likely to be the case by only offering to give attention when you initiate it. This does not mean that you or your dog will have to go without. You can give it as much fuss as you want if your dog is relaxed, i.e. not seeking attention when you start to give it. However if your dog is seeking attention, do not tell it to go away because this in itself would be a response. If your dog keeps nudging you, just look away and fold your arms. If your dog tries to climb on you, quietly push it off.

Too Close for Comfort

Allowing your dog to sit on your lap or next to you on the furniture increases physical contact, which may contrast too greatly with your absence. It will also reinforce anxiety if your dog needs to get on your lap, so it is advantageous to prevent this possibility by not letting your dog sit on you. A variant on this theme is to adopt a policy of only allowing your dog to sit on your lap when you invite it to.

Counter-Conditioning

It is important that certain actions which cause your dog to become anxious because they are associated with your departure, such as you putting your coat on, are associated with your presence.

250

2.   Learning to be Alone

Accustom your dog to periods of time when it is separated from you when you are at home and awake. If you do not give your dog the run of the house when you are out, try to use the area in which you want your dog to stay. This process will provide your dog with an experience that is intermediate between being with you all the time and your total absence.

If you use a child-gate to start with, you will avoid the stress that may be caused if you just closed the door. Accustoming your dog to a closed door is something you can progress towards. If necessary you may have to approach this whole area in the same way as moving a dog out of the bedroom (see *Sleeping Arrangements* below.)

Some time separated from you on a Sunday can be a good idea if you are due to work on Monday. Interestingly, a number of owners who work **9-5** Monday to Friday report that their dog's separation problem is worse at the beginning of the week than it is towards the weekend.

As a practitioner I have noticed a high incidence of separation problems in dogs whose owners work shifts and those who work from home most of the time, but go out for meetings occasionally. If I am right, this could be because their dogs find an inability to predict what will happen in their environment stressful. If this applies to you, replicating periods of separation when you are actually at home may be helpful.

3.   Sleeping Arrangements

Allowing your dog to sleep in the bedroom, or on the bed, may encourage it to become overly attached to you. There will certainly be a big contrast between this and your absence if you go to work in the morning. Place a child-gate across your open bedroom door so that your dog can see in but cannot get in. Once your dog has become accustomed to this you can gradually, over several weeks, move the gate further away until your dog is sleeping in the kitchen or in some other convenient location. A gradual weaning process is beneficial because it avoids making your dog stressful and prevents sleepless nights caused by it whining, barking etc.

This process is even better if it is carried out in reverse, which a few clients have opted for or have needed to do. Their dog slept in the kitchen behind a child-gate whilst they slept the other side on a camp bed. Once their dogs seemed relaxed about this arrangement the owners moved their bed a little further away each night until they were sleeping out of sight, and finally they returned to sleeping in their own bedroom.

Things To Do In All Cases

Emotional Goodbyes

Your behaviour as you leave the house can make a big difference to your dog's state of mind if it is prone to separation anxiety, or is overly dependent on your presence due to fear, because the contrast between a high-profile departure and one that is more relaxed is quite significant. Introducing these techniques should help you avoid unwittingly reinforcing anxiety.

The best approach is to cool your relationship towards your dog, becoming less affectionate about an hour before you leave so that it is less likely that your dog will want to be with you when you go.

Option A: About half an hour before you are due to leave, separate your dog from you by putting it in the area that it has become accustomed to being left in for periods of time when you are at home.

Option B: If your dog is not used to having its liberty restricted to one part of the house during your absence, simply reduce its opportunity to follow you about the house for the remainder of this half hour.

Options A and B: Prepare to leave the house by putting on your coat and shoes etc. and pick up your car keys, but do not leave immediately. This will have the effect of disassociating the sight and sound of these activities from your imminent departure. There is nothing in dog language for *'Bye bye, Be a good boy. Mummy will see you later.'* Any interaction when you leave the house is likely to reinforce any anxiety your dog is feeling, so simply close the door behind you without saying "Goodbye". When you return, adopt a matter of fact attitude, and only give affection once your dog has calmed down.

Comforters

Leaving your dog with things it associates with relaxation will help it to settle. Rawhide chews, bones and chew toys such as a Kong that can be filled with food are a good idea, but impregnate them with your scent first. Storing them with your unwashed laundry should achieve this. Impregnating some of your dog's bedding or an old towel in the same way will allow your dog to lie in a pool of your scent for security. This is only effective however if the clothes have been freshly impregnated. Giving your dog your old jumper and leaving it on its bed forever will not be effective beyond the first day.

If you are concerned about dog hair transferring to your clothing, you can keep the cloth in a bag made of a material that will allow the scent to permeate through but prevent dog hair from escaping. Every time you leave, you should place a cloth, freshly impregnated with your scent, on your dog's bed or other area it likes to lie in during your absence. If applicable, you can place another scent-impregnated cloth along the bottom of the door that would give your dog access to you, such as the kitchen door. The cloth should be placed on your side, so that when your dog sniffs at the door your scent will be very strong. This will not cause your dog to think you are still at home, but it might provide some comfort.

If your dog's separation problem is caused by fear, keep a cloth for scent impregnation as above but instead of placing a cloth *in* your dog's bed, place it *in front* of your dog's bed, or in front of the areas in which it likes to lie, so as to create a form of scent barrier behind which it can feel secure.

If your dog is very stressed you will find it will not chew any of the food items you leave it with until you get home; but they should be put in place every time you leave, so that it has the option. To maintain the novelty of these items they should only be left out when your dog is left unattended: but, to prevent them being a clue to your impending departure and consequently inducing stress, adopt the practice of giving these items to your dog when it is separated from you whilst you are at home. If your dog will eat them it will be relaxed and this will go some way in helping to associate relaxation with your absence.

You and your family can make tape recordings of your voices quietly talking. The tape recording should be as long as possible. If your tapes are limited to forty-five minutes, they will still be useful because anxiety is at its peak in the first half an hour of owner absence. Once you have made your tape recording, start it just before you leave. It is not necessary that the tape recorder is played in the room where your dog is being left. In fact it is probably preferable not to have the dog and tape in the same room together, if your dog has become accustomed to being left in the kitchen or utility room whilst you are in the living room. Although the sound of your voice(s) will not cause your dog to believe that you are still at home, it should have the effect of helping it to remain relaxed. As with the chew items mentioned above, it is important that the tape recording does not become a clue that tells your dog that it is being left. To prevent this, play the tape every now and again when you are at home.

Leaving a radio or television on for a distressed dog is often suggested. This is a good idea if your dog is used to the radio or television running fairly constantly when you are at home, because it will be a clue associated with your presence and relaxation.

Drug Support

Drug support can be useful as an aid to treating some forms of separation anxiety.[12] However drug support is not necessary in the majority of cases, especially if the problem is mild. Of course, the inclusion of drug support will be dependent upon your vet's opinion and an accurate diagnosis of the cause of the symptoms.

Other Causes of Separation Problems

Attention-Seeking

Responding positively to your dog by telling it off when it barks, yaps or scratches at a door to get your attention when you are at home may be seen by your dog as 'rewarding' it. If this pattern of behaviour is repeated and becomes established when you are at home such as once you have gone to bed, the behaviour may be exhibited with even greater force when your dog is left, because this is the way it has learned to get attention. The fact that someone comes back eventually may reinforce the behaviour because it seems to have been successful.

Boredom

If you think your dog's separation problem is caused by boredom you can leave it with things to keep it occupied and to help it settle. These can include rawhide chews, a sterilised bone, a Kong (a toy) with a biscuit wedged in it, a food dispensing Buster Cube or its equivalent. The important thing is to make sure that your dog finds the item(s) interesting and stress-relieving. The best way to do this is to maintain their novelty value and only let your dog have them when you are about to leave, and remove them when you come home. Before you adopt this policy however, encourage your dog to try and get the food out of the toy, or demolish the chew on several occasions, generating as much excitement as you can, so as to help ensure your dog's interest in them. However if you find that your dog shows no interest in food items when it is left alone but eats them as soon as you get home, it is probably so stressed that it loses its appetite, and the problem is not simply boredom.

Displaced Aggression

If you think that your dog's separation problems are caused by it redirecting its territorial aggression onto items inside your home, e.g. by grabbing a cushion and giving it a good shake, you will have to address the root cause of the problem. The same rule applies if you think that a separation problem is being made worse by your dog's sense of dominance and its frustration at being left by its pack.

How long is too long?

The length of time you can leave your dog depends on the environment, the individual and its previous experience. For example, a dog that has access to a secure garden, via a dog flap, can be left for longer periods than a dog that is shut in one room.

Feeding and Exercise

Your dog may be more settled if it has an appropriate amount of exercise. However, the exercise period should not be too close to the time you leave the house. It may also be more inclined to settle if it has been fed before it is left.

Ineffective Punishment:

One of the most common factors that causes all separation problems to worsen is the owner's response if they find their dog has made a mess or been destructive in their absence. It may be tempting to punish your dog if you come home to find your room looking a mess, but your dog can only link its actions with the consequences of its actions if they occur within half a second of each other. So your dog will see your anger as unprovoked aggression, and will behave submissively when you arrive. Humans often interpret this as a sign of guilt - which it isn't. Apart from being terribly unfair, this also makes the dog anxious about what its owners will do when they come home the next time it is left, which means it is more likely to chew or lose toilet control, and the problem spirals out of control (also see Chapter 4).

If you do arrive home to find your dog has been destructive or made a mess, smile sweetly and quietly put your dog outside, or in another room and then clear up. When you have finished, bang your head against a wall. It will make you feel a whole lot better and prevent you from exacerbating the problem by losing your temper with your dog. Then sit down and contemplate what could be causing the problem.

Jealousy

Some patterns of dog behaviour are occasionally described as jealousy by their owners. It could be argued that jealousy is an emotion that requires a cognitive ability which dogs are not capable of; conversely it could be argued that jealousy in dogs is part of a range of emotions that includes wanting another dog's bone. An obvious example of such behaviour is the rivalry between two or more dogs for their owner's attention: some couples complain that their dog will get between them when they kiss, cuddle or even touch each other.

Owner attention is a resource dogs may compete for. Loss of this resource seems to trigger aggression, something fundamental to a dog's emotional state.[13] The complexity of the behaviour is reflected in the fact that some dogs will react aggressively when their owner's attention or presence is about to be withdrawn. Classic examples of this occur when the owner tries to leave the house, attempts to answer the phone or hang up the washing. In some cases the dog's behaviour may have started as an attention-seeking device such as barking, chasing after the owner or nipping at them. In other cases such a development process does not seem to occur and the dog's distress or frustration is the only trigger of the aggressive response. Even when status-related aggression is displayed, there is also an underlying tendency to anxiety or fear that a resource may be lost to another.

In all cases it is important to look at what can be done to reduce a dog's over-dependence on it's owners and on receiving their attention (see Ch. 16). If necessary, this often needs to be combined with changing the dog's perception of its high status within the family/pack so as to increase its inhibition about displaying aggression towards family members (see p. 172). The aggressive behaviour itself may have to be inhibited (see ch. 5), but in most cases, counter-conditioning the dog's emotional response to the things that signal the withdrawal of owner attention is a more appropriate course of action (see Ch.13 for the principles of counter-conditioning). Whatever approach is used, it is a good idea to set up training situations under the guidance of a pet behaviour counsellor.

NOTES

1. McCrave, E.A. "Diagnostic Criteria for Separation Anxiety in the Dog" Veterinary Clinics of North America: Small Animal Practice Vol 21, No 2, March 1991.

2. Mugford R.A. 1995 Canine Behavioural Therapy from Serpell J. (Ed.) The Domestic Dog. Cambridge University Press.

3. As 1.

4. Dorland's Pocket Medical Dictionary 1989 W.B. Saunders Co

5. Overall, K. L. 1997 Clinical Behavioral Medicine for Small Animals. Mosby. St. Louis. Missoury.

6. McBride, E.A., Bradshaw, J.W.S., Christians, A., McPherson, J and Bailey, G. "Factors Predisposing dogs to Separation Problems" found in Rutter, Rushen, Randle and Eddison (ed) Proceedings of the 29th International Congress of the International Society for Applied Ethology" Universities Federation for Animal Welfare, 1995.

7. Serpell. J.A. & Jagoe. A. 1995. Early experience and the development of behaviour. In; Serpell, J.A. (Ed) The Domestic Dog; Its Evolution, Behaviour and Interactions With People. Cambridge University Press.

8. As 1.

9. Sautter, F.J. & Glover, J.A. 1978 Behaviour, Development and Training of the Dog. Arco Publishing Company Inc.

10. Holmes, R. 1993 "Separation Anxiety & Grieving by Dogs and Cats" p211 of Animal Behaviour (The TG Hungerford Refresher Course for Veterinarians Proceedings 214), Post Graduate Committee in Veterinary Science, University of Sydney.

11. As 9.

12. In a double-blinded, placebo trial, Novartis Animal Health investigated the role of pharmacology and behavioural modification techniques in the treatment of separation-related anxiety in dogs, i.e. overattachment. The main finding was that the use of the optimum dose of the drug used in the trial, Clomipramine, in combination with behaviour modification caused a greater frequency of improvement, or disappearance, of the

signs of separation related anxiety than the combination of behaviour modification and placebo. This was significant over the first two months, after which behaviour modification and placebo drew level in terms of the results achieved. The implication of this is that owners can have some relief from the symptoms of separation anxiety whilst implementing the behaviour modification programme.

13.   Fox, M.W. *Understanding Your Dog* (Coward, McCann and Geoghegan Inc., N.Y., 1972)

—17.—

Driving you Crazy!
Difficult Behaviour in the Car

Does your car rock from side to side as your dog does figure of eights in the back?

Do your windows vibrate with the sound of incessant barking?

Various things motivate dogs to bark while they are in their owner's car. Some dogs are simply excited because they anticipate reaching a pleasant destination, such as the park. One owner of a noisy German Shepherd dog once passed me a pair of industrial ear defenders - the

261

type usually worn by tractor drivers - as I got into his car. When I incredulously enquired whether this was normal procedure, he assured me that he and his family wore them on every trip!

Dogs easily work themselves into a frenzy of excited anticipation, but if the car moves away from familiar territory, they tend to settle down. However as soon as the dog suspects the journey is coming to an end, it will spring to its feet and start getting excited again. Efforts to get the dog back under control are often futile, because each journey terminates at an exciting destination. To the dog, any shouting from its owners makes it seem as if they are joining in with its excitement, and consequently all the occupants of the car human and canine are often seen progressing down the road 'barking' together. It is significant that these dogs are unlikely to bark on the way home.

A more obscure reason why dogs become frantic in the car is herding or hunting behaviour. This is most commonly seen in Border Collies, which can become obsessed with the back-seat 'chasing' of any vehicles - such as motorbikes - that dare to pass their owner's car. Some even try to 'chase' stationary objects, because the action of the car passing gives an impression of movement. Dogs which demonstrate this behaviour are easily identified because they spend every journey with their noses pressed against the side windows waiting for the next chance to chase something. However, all but the most obsessed dogs will settle down on the motorway, because the closest vehicles are moving in the same direction and are consequently far less exciting.

Territorial aggression or aggression caused by fear, or a mixture of both, can stimulate a similar pattern of behaviour. These are particularly likely to occur in urban areas where people and other dogs can get quite close to the car.

Some dogs bark in the car to get their owner's attention. Travelling is an unique experience for most of these dogs because it is the only circumstance where they are expected to sit and look at the back of their owner's head. If the dog is used to receiving attention on demand at home, it can't understand why it is being ignored, and tries to regain the owner's attention by barking.

This is most likely to occur if the dog has a tendency to display attention-seeking behaviour at home as well. Owners who shout back are unwittingly giving the dog the attention he wants, which encourages the dog to bark again. Attention seekers typically face the front of the car to 'talk' to their owners, and show no real interest in what is going on outside.

A variation of this behaviour is seen when the dog wants to sit in the front of the car rather than in the back. This often starts in puppyhood because owners allow their cute little puppy to sit on a passenger's lap, but once the dog grows up this is no longer convenient. When the owners try to persuade their dog to sit in the back it may start to complain because it has become used to sitting in the front and won't settle for anything less.

Applying the Brakes.

Defusing hysterical travelling dogs is a gradual process. In order to achieve some peace, you should increasingly make trips that don't end with your dog enjoying a free run. For example, your dog could be taken to the petrol station or the local shops, or even just round the block without getting out of the car. Eventually these mundane trips will start to balance out the exciting ones, and your dog should become a calmer traveller.

When you reach your destination, keep your dog in the car until it has quietened down. This will help to prevent the development of an

263

association between excitement and being let out, which might otherwise reinforce the excitable behaviour.

Reducing a dog's excitability about an anticipated destination can be taken one stage further. Every time the dog becomes excited, pull over and stop the car. Only when your dog has become calm should you move off again. In practice, this technique does work, but it requires consistency and dedication, and extreme patience on the part of your other passengers! Special trips for training purposes are advisable. Your dog will eventually learn that the way to keep the car moving is to stay quiet.

Simple Silencers

Dogs that bark at things they see from the car windows can be tethered so that they have to lie down below window level in the rear of your car (if you have a hatchback or an estate). The lead (which should be attached to your dog's collar - not a check chain) should be short enough to enable your dog to lie down comfortably, but not long enough to enable it to sit up fully. This will encourage your dog to keep lying down. Apart from not getting excited at other vehicles on the road, because they now can't be seen, lying down is also a subordinate body posture for the dog, which may make it less inclined to take the initiative to bark.

This is also a much safer position: in a head-on crash the dog will be safely restrained against the back of the rear seat. Without a firm dog guard, it could otherwise fly over the top of the seats and either break the neck of the person in front or go through the windscreen. There is also the possibility that a loose dog may attempt to guard the car while rescuers are trying to get unconscious passengers out.

Tethering is also useful for dogs who bark to get their owner's attention because the dog can no longer see the back of its owner's head. The owner can then speak to the dog quietly when it is not demanding attention, to reinforce good behaviour. Adopting this policy at home can also help. If progress is slow, a passenger can make a habit of sitting in a position where they can feed your dog a small tit-bit as a reward when it is quiet, to reinforce good behaviour. It shouldn't take your dog long to realise that the way to get these rewards is to keep quiet.

In some extreme cases, the barking for attention can be resolved in the short term by letting your dog sit in the front footwell of the car - on the passenger's side, of course! There will still be enough room for a passenger as well. Your dog will have to be tethered for safety's sake, or its lead held by the passenger.

Obviously starting how you mean to go on is the best way to prevent problems occurring. Be brave, and ensure your new puppy becomes accustomed to travelling in the back of the car when it is first collected from the breeder, rather than on someone's lap.

However, if you think your dog's problem is related to fear, attention-seeking or territorial behaviour, you should refer to the relevant section of this book.

—— 18. ——

Physiological Aspects of Behaviour

The Implications of Diet

Diet has a direct effect on behaviour. If a dog eats too much it will become obese and lethargic. If a dog is hungry, it may become a scavenger, steal food or become coprophagic (see page 269). To ensure that your dog has an adequate and well-balanced diet, discuss the matter with your vet.

A properly fed dog is more likely to be content. If given the opportunity, dogs will eat several small meals during the day. This preference can be usefully exploited when feeding dogs that show increasing aggression when they are woken from a state of deep sleep following a heavy meal.

Owners often claim that their dog is hyperactive and blame the cause on its diet. However, such 'hyperactivity' is often nothing more than a pattern of behaviour that has become established (and reinforced by the owners response), or the consequence of a lack of exercise. A truly hyperactive dog is likely to be unable to settle in all circumstances, and will show physiological symptoms such as an increased heart rate. If you truly believe that your dog falls into this category you should consult your vet, because the symptoms you are observing may have an underlying medical cause.[1]

There is nevertheless some evidence to show that sensitivity to a particular diet can be the cause of some behaviour problems. For example, dietary sensitivity has been identified as possible cause of unpredictable aggressive behaviour in some Golden Retrievers[2]. If you want to eliminate the possibility of certain foods acting as the trigger for your dog's behaviour, discuss the matter with your vet. He or she may advise you to try an exclusion diet for a few weeks, such as fish and potato, or chicken, rice and green vegetables. If you find that the problem is resolved, you can work out together which diet will be suitable for your dog.

If things settle down for a while and problems recur at a later date you will have to consider the possibility that your dog has become sensitised to the new diet and an alternative may have to be found. As before you should seek guidance.

Many owners find themselves changing their dog's diet from one type to another in an attempt to find one that will suit it and will not cause diarrhoea. These conditions are often attributable to diet and gastro-enterinal problems, about which again you should consult your vet. They can also be symptomatic of stress and anxiety. If your vet thinks this is the case, it may be of greater value, and better for your dog's welfare, if you address the cause of the problem rather than tinker with the symptoms by changing the diet.

A lot has been written about diets which are too high in protein affecting a dog's behaviour, and consequently many owners try feeding their dog a low protein food. However there is a lot of confusion about the subject and what actually constitutes a low protein diet. The information provided on bags of dry complete dog food quote protein levels at around **16-24%**. At first glance this seems high when compared with tins of dog food that typically give figures of around **8%**. What you have to bear in mind is the fact that the tinned food can contain anything between **60%** and **80%** of water. This means that the protein level is higher when seen as a percentage of dried matter if the water is taken out.

Recent research in America[3] has shown that there is a correlation between high protein diets and a high incidence of territorial aggression, motivated by fear. This may imply that there is an influence on aggression caused by fear in other situations as well.

The whys and wherefores of high protein diets

Tryptophan is an amino acid naturally occurring in the diet. It is necessary to the production of serotonin, synthesised within the neurons of the dog's nervous system. Serotonin controls the balance of a dog's mood: too little in the diet can cause depression and anxiety, but also possibly sexual and other aggression, increased appetite and restlessness and lack of sleep. Tryptophan has to compete for transport across the blood-brain barrier with other amino acids found in protein. Therefore a diet that is overly rich in protein can 'crowd out' tryptophan from the dog's brain, detrimentally affecting the synthesis of serotonin and thereby adversely affecting the dog's behaviour.

It has also been suggested that by increasing the dog's carbohydrate intake (and monitoring vitamin B6), certain behaviour problems, such as fear in dogs may be improved. An increase in brain serotonin levels may reduce reactivity and improve learning and decision making, thus aiding the success of other behavioural techniques.

If, in consultation with your vet, you decide on this course of action, establish a balanced diet: increase additional carbohydrate intake proportionally, such as two additional separate feeds of wholemeal pasta. One feed for average-sized dogs, such as a Labrador or Collie, is about a dessert bowlful. A saucerful should suit small dogs. If necessary, increase Vitamin B6 intake by giving brewer's yeast tablets. Throughout such a dietary project, it would be very helpful to keep a diary so as to monitor your dog's behaviour.

Coprophagia

The subject of dogs that eat their own - or other dogs - faeces, is something that we do not like to talk about. However our sensitivity is not shared by coprophagic dogs! This is a common problem, possibly an evolutionary hang-over from those dog ancestors that scavenged around man's dwellings.

This behaviour is normal and allows food absorption to be maximised, which would have a survival value in times of hardship in the wild. For some species, such as rabbits, eating their faeces is the necessary secondary stage of the way food is digested. In dogs and some other mammals, the behaviour is also seen as a manifestation of the maternal instinct for nest cleaning and licking immobile puppies to cause defecation and urination, the results of which are consumed.

Why certain dogs indulge in the habit of coprophagia despite the fact that their owners provide them with food has been the subject of debate. Some explanations suggest dietary deficiency, or a result of a learnt behaviour developed during a period of boredom, such as

269

during prolonged kennelling in puppyhood. Certainly, a significantly high incidence has been found in dogs that have had to fend for themselves, such as strays[4]. Sometimes the faeces seem to have food value because of the richness of the depositor's diet.

Various ways of overcoming the problem by altering what a dog eats have been suggested. These include changing the diet to one of the premium dried foods. These are processed more easily by the dog's body before being passed, and it will find the resultant faeces less appealing.

Various additions to the diet are also thought to be helpful, such as pineapple chunks because of the presence of an enzyme that aids digestion. Adding **10%** fibre to the diet may also be helpful: this can be achieved by using a bulkier dry diet, or by adding fibrous material such as bran or boiled green vegetables to the normal diet.

If your dog has a coprophagic habit you should discuss the dietary aspects of this antisocial behaviour in more detail with your vet, who will also be able to exclude physical causes for the behaviour (an important step, particularly if the onset is sudden), and can prescribe some additives for your dog's diet that will make its own faeces less palatable.

Whatever the cause of the behaviour it is often developed into a worse problem by the owner's response. For example their understandable dislike of their dog's habit may cause them to rush out into the garden with spade in hand to clear up before their dog can eat what it has passed. From the dog's point of view this may look like competition, and some dogs become so determined to beat their owners to it that they will eat their faeces as soon as it has been excreted!

The best way to prevent this is to make the act of toileting a prelude to something more interesting to your dog than eating what it has just deposited. When you let your dog into your garden or yard, stand near a window in a position where your dog is unable to see you. When your dog relieves itself open the door that will allow it to re-enter your home, and as soon as it arrives give it a titbit reward or some of its daily food allowance, then leave it indoors while you clear the ground outside. After a few repetitions of this your dog should anticipate that as soon as it has relieved itself the door will open and it will receive food, thus replacing its interest in what is lying on the ground behind it.

Of course, you should not let your dog out under these circumstances if you are unable to supervise, unless it is muzzled (see page.232). If your dog has already developed a tendency to eat its faeces as soon as there is any chance that someone may try and clear it up, you may first have to teach it that the sound of the door opening means something pleasant will follow when it enters. Choose times when your dog has not just that minute defecated. This method will result in your dog receiving several small meals a day, which in itself is a means of addressing the problem because the dog's interest in faeces as a source food should, with luck, be reduced.

If your dog eats the faeces of other dogs away from home, the problem may be more difficult to solve. Some owners have to rely on the use of a muzzle whenever it is let off the lead. Whenever possible, dogs that are coprophagic should be walked where the faeces of other dogs are unlikely to occur. In many cases, however, modifying the behaviour can be achieved by repeatedly approaching faeces with your dog on a lead, extending lead or long line, and using the training discs, rattle can, etc. to inhibit your dog's approach behaviour.

Eventually your dog should become suspicious that the training discs or rattle can will arrive as it shows interest in faeces, and will avoid them. It is important that you use these techniques to stop your dog from approaching the items, because the effectiveness of the learning will be reduced significantly if they arrive after it has started to consume them. You can also use the *"off"* technique and clicker training as a means of developing and reinforcing appropriate behaviour (see separate entries for all of these).

A paper[5] presented at the first **International Conference on Veterinary Behavioural Medicine** in **1997** discussed the effectiveness of a remote controlled collar that ejects compressed air at the ground as a means of inhibiting dogs from picking up food bits left on the ground. This was found to be highly successful as a means of reducing the dogs interest in the food baits the researchers had left out. Should such a device ever become commercially available it would have an obvious application as a means of inhibiting coprophagia.

Sometimes the use of taste deterrents, such as tabasco sauce or chilli powder, is advocated as a means of putting a dog off. The idea is to sprinkle the faeces with these so that the dog finds the sensation in its mouth unpleasant when it eats them. This is often unsuccessful because dogs have relatively little sense of taste, and their sense of smell allows them to identify which faeces to avoid.

As a final resort to be used only in the most serious cases, dogs can be deterred form eating faeces by giving them an emetic[6] (something to make them sick). This should be timed so that an association is formed causing the dog to avoid faeces in the future. Of course this approach requires veterinary involvement and guidance from a behaviour counsellor.

Physical problems and behaviour

Dogs change their normal behaviour when they are ill or in pain, therefore it is important to rule out this possibility before you embark on a course of training to alter your dog's behaviour - apart from problems of general control. If a dog is ill, and this is not identified, it could be harmed by the introduction of inappropriate treatment.

This is particularly relevant if its behaviour involves a sudden onset of aggression. For example, attempting to modify aggressive behaviour by using conditioned avoidance or aversion therapy to treat a dog's aggressive response to everyday stimuli would be inappropriate if the dog's behaviour is caused by episodic discontrol, a sub-epileptic condition. Such attempts could be stressful for the dog and aggravate the condition. Another rare cause of a low threshold of aggression is associated with hepatic encephalopathy (a misfunction of the liver).

Sometimes treatment for a physical condition has to be introduced by the vet before behaviour modification can begin. For example, you may need to counter-condition your dog's fear of being touched near its ear which is resulting in defensive behaviour, but there is no point in starting until the cause of the pain has been treated.

I recently treated a case where a dog growled at its owners when they put its food down for it, but not in defence of its food. This was originally caused by a split tooth that caused pain when the dog ate, and anticipation of the pain triggered the dog's defensive behaviour. Luckily the vet was able to identify and treat the problem before work began to stop the dog's learnt behaviour of growling. If the tooth had not been treated, it would probably have been impossible to treat the behaviour, however hard we tried.

On another occasion, a Dachshund that snapped at its owners during handling was referred to me. The behaviour modification programme did not prove successful and further veterinary investigation was instigated, which revealed that a spinal injury was causing pain during handling. Another case involved a rescued Old English Sheepdog that snapped at its new owners when they attempted to stroke it. I was suspicious that the dog was startled by things suddenly coming into view, and referred the clients back to their vet. My suspicion was confirmed when the dog was found to have progressive retinal atrophy, a condition that results in tunnel vision.

When examining your dog, the vet will be able to advise you if the problem warrants referral to a pet behaviour counsellor for more detailed guidance, in preference to trying a self-help approach. Your vet will also decide if certain fear- or anxiety-related conditions require drug support before any behaviour modification training is begun.

Exercise and Behaviour

A lack of exercise and mental stimulation is not only unhealthy for your dog; it can also exacerbate existing behaviour problems, or trigger new ones. What constitutes a suitable level of exercise obviously varies according to the quality of the exercise and the type of dog. Your dog expends far more energy running up and down a hillside than strolling through a park on a lead.

Neutering

Vets and pet behaviour counsellors sometimes recommend neutering to help cure certain behaviour problems in dogs and bitches. These familiar problems include aggression towards other dogs or members of the owner's family, frequent masturbation against objects or even the legs of visitors, or roaming away to find mates. It is also a realistic policy adopted by many rescue organisations to prevent unwanted litters. According to the gender of the owner, however, castration is often an emotive issue. Many female owners subscribe to the idea with ready ease, but the majority of male owners are most reluctant to consider such an operation, despite all the evidence and logical arguments in favour. Oddly enough they are often quite happy for bitches and female cats to be spayed...

Neutering male dogs (castration)

Sometimes owners are reluctant to neuter their dog because they know someone whose dog was castrated but its behaviour did not improve. Sadly there are occasions when this does occur, but normally because the operation was not appropriate in the circumstances. An owner may be led to believe that castration would modify the dog's aggression towards people and other dogs, but they will be disappointed if the aggression is actually motivated by fear, which is not a testosterone-related problem. Accurate diagnosis is therefore essential to determine whether castration is appropriate.

Castration is most likely to be of help in cases of problem behaviour that are more common in one sex than another. Males exhibit behaviours which are influenced by testosterone: scent marking, leaving home to find mates, inappropriate sexual and scent marking behaviour, aggression displayed towards other male dogs, and rank-related aggression between dogs within the family (see Chapter 12). Castration can also help in some cases that are not gender specific, such as status-related aggression in the household, because removing the influence of testosterone improves the dog's control of aggression.

Even when castration is appropriate, it is not a certain cure.[7] Success varies from 90% for some problems, such as roaming to find potential mates, down to 50% for others such as inappropriate scent marking. This is because the dog's brain is programmed to display male behaviour by testosterone even before birth. If castration has been recommended, the chances of success are always greatly improved if the operation is carried out in conjunction with behaviour modification therapy.

One of the arguments against castration is that it is unnatural. This is true, but we expect our dogs to live in what is for them an unnatural world. They are subjected to pressures they would not encounter if they were running wild like their cousin the wolf. For example, it would be natural for packs of wolves to attack any other wolves they encounter on their territory. Although a dog still has many of the wolf's instinctive drives, it is expected to accept all the male dogs it meets in the park quite happily.

It is also natural for males to mark their territory with scent by leaving droplets of urine in prominent places, such as trees, but it is extremely annoying for owners and visitors if the dog develops the habit inside the house! It is also natural for dogs to compete with other pack members for the right to mate and pass on its genes. However, things can get difficult if this competition is directed at male dogs or male members of the family.

A reluctance to castrate is very understandable in dog owners, who would often like their pets to breed. However, breeding should not be undertaken lightly - there are enough unwanted dogs as it is. Certainly, mating should never be allowed in the hope that relieving the dog's frustrations will cure his behavioural problems. Once he has had experience of mating, some behaviour problems are likely to increase, not decrease.

Perhaps the fact that most dogs are not allowed to mate for fear of creating unwanted puppies is the most convincing argument for the routine neutering of dogs. An un-neutered male can lead a frustrated life, especially if he is likely to encounter the smell of bitches on heat. Surely it is better to save him that agony. After all, if he has never

276

read Playdog, he won't know what he's missing!

Neutering Females (spaying)

The idea of neutering bitches normally meets with less resistance than the subject of neutering males. There are the health benefits of a considerably reduced risk of the development of mammary tumours later in life if a bitch is neutered when she is young. The risk of pyometra (a life-threatening infection of the uterus that can occur in maiden bitches, particularly in later life) is also removed. The risk of an unwanted pregnancy and the inconvenience of bleeding during each oestrus (season) is removed. Spaying also removes the difficulty of having male dogs follow you home every time you take your bitch out for a walk when she is in season. It will, however, increase the tendency for a bitch to put on weight because of an increase in appetite, but this will not occur if the food you give her is proportionate to the exercise she gets. Consider the fact that all working guide dogs are neutered and yet they are not allowed to get overweight.

Spaying may also be appropriate if a bitch's season brings on specific problems, such as the adoption of items as surrogate puppies, nest building and the onset of aggression over items the bitch may identify as resources. The critical times include the period before a bitch's season, (pro-oestrus) and after it, when for a while she will be affected by hormonal changes associated with false pregnancy.

It is important to be aware that the dog is descended from a species in which, in a stable group, a dominant female can subjugate her subordinates, and compete for resources and the attentions of the males in such a way that these subordinates will not breed. However if rivals do breed, serious conflict can follow. It has been suggested that neutering will not immediately remove the aggression associated with a bitch's oestrous cycle. The recurrence of this problem may continue for two or three cycles after a bitch has been spayed. There has been some interesting research on the effects of spaying on bitches that are showing aggression .[8]

Hormone Treatments

Males

Hormone treatments are sometimes recommended as a means of controlling certain behaviour problems. In males, synthetic hormones or hormone inhibitors can be given in the form of tablets or injections. These treatments can give owners a breathing space in which to treat behaviour problems without resorting to castration.

A hormone treatment can also be used to indicate whether neutering or castration is appropriate. However, as these treatments have a calming effect on the nervous system as well as altering the hormone balance, it is not always clear whether the resulting improvement in behaviour is due to interfering with the hormone levels at all. This makes the behavioural outcome of neutering less easy to predict.

Females

Hormone treatments are available which can stop a bitch coming into season. This also prevents the associated behaviour problems before and after her season. These treatments also seem to work with bitches that have been spayed but still show aggression in keeping with their oestrus cycle.

Appetite

Some hormone treatments increase appetite. If the dog begins to develop problems such as guarding or stealing food, you should consult your vet.

NOTES

1. Overall, K.L. *Clinical Behaviour Medicine for Small Animals*. (Mosby. St. Louis, Missoury 1997)

2. Lindsey, S. *Dietary Hypersensitivity and Behaviour - Fact or Fad?* (Companion Animal Study Group, Newsletter. Summer 1995)

3. Dodman, N.H. *Effect of dietary protein content on behaviour*. **Journal of the American Veterinary Association** Vol. 208 No 3 p376-379, 1996

4. Serpell, J.A. & Jagoe, A. *Early experience and the development of behaviour*. In Serpell, J.A. (Ed.) The Domestic Dog; Its Evolution, Behaviour and Interactions With People. (Cambridge University Press 1995)

5. Pageat, P., Tessier, Y. *Evaluation of the efficiency of a remote controlled spray collar in modification of an unwanted behaviour - picking up food baits*. (Proceedings of the First International Conference on Veterinary Behavioural Medicine. Universities Federation for Animal Welfare. Potters Bar, Great Britain. 1997)

6. Mugford R. A. *Canine Behavioural Therapy* from Serpell J. (Ed.) The Domestic Dog (Cambridge University Press 1995)

7. Hopkins, S.G., Schubert, T.A. and Hart, B.L. *Castration of Male Dogs: Effects on roaming, aggression, urine marking and mounting*. **Journal of the American Veterinary Association**. 168 1108, 1976

8. Research at Edinburgh University has shown that if a bitch shows aggression before she is spayed, the problem may be harder to treat than if she is left unspayed. The researchers recommended that problems of aggression are treated before spaying is considered. They did not, however consider the specific problem of bitches that are only aggressive around the time of their season.

    O'Farrell, V. and Peachey E. *Behavioural effects of ovariohysterectomy in bitches*. **Journal of Small Animal Practise** 31:595-598, 1990

About the Illustrator

Drew Marland spent some time in the drawing office of HM Dockyard, Portsmouth, before running away to sea, where he took several years furthering an early enthusiasm for things that go bang, working on seismic survey ships. After a run of North Sea winters and wet boots, he moved downstairs to the engine rooms where it is always nice and warm. He swallowed the anchor in time to greet the arrival of his daughter this year, and aspires to cosy domesticity, complicated only by the vagaries of his dogs, viz.:

Bessie, a Border Collie, whose known history began when she was found tied to a gate post in deepest Herefordshire. After a spell in two rescue homes, she was adopted by Drew's wife Pip in **1989**. Bessie has one blue and one brown eye, has the usual highly-strung temperament of her breed, and hates things that go bang.

Gromit, a Lurcher with presumed Greyhound and Wolfhound ancestry, came from the Bristol Dogs Home in **1993**. Of a lugubrious disposition, he radiates angst, an air of tragedy and a wide assortment of odours. He is periodically animated by the appearance of creatures which he defines as quarry, and will pursue them until the expiry or exhaustion of one or the other. This can be, and often is, inconvenient. He is a prime candidate for tuition by this book.

Billy came from a Dogs' Home in the Welsh valleys a day before he was due to be put down. A rescue worker on one of her regular trips from Bristol was loading up her car with canine rejects when she found she had room for one small extra. Billy clips down to a neat terrier size and was squeezed in. He hates strangers, other dogs (especially bigger ones - i.e. most of them) and motorbikes, will eat your biscuit if you don't guard it, and is another case in need of reform.

Drew Marland can be contacted at **6 Belvedere Rd., Bristol BS6 Tel. 0117 9733575**

Further Help

Pet Behaviour Counselling.

The profession of pet behaviour counselling has changed over the years. When I saw my first case in **1986** the idea that an understanding of ethology (the study of animals in their normal environment), psychology, learning theory, neurology, pharmacology, and the implementation of counselling skills could help people cure problem behaviours in pets was not new to British shores. But the general public need for behaviour counselling, and the efficacy of treatment, were not as readily recognised by the veterinary profession and the pet-owning public as they are today.

The APBC

The Association of Pet Behaviour Counsellors was formed in **1989**. Apart from promoting pet behaviour generally, the aim of the association was to set out criteria for membership and codes of practice that would allow vets to refer their cases of pet behavioural problems to the APBC with confidence. Some readers might question why it is necessary for owners to be referred by a vet. The reason is that a significant proportion of behaviour problems have a medical cause, and these must be excluded prior to therapy. There is now a special interest group for vets, the Companion Animal Behaviour Therapy Study Group (CABTSG), to which most APBC members also belong.

The APBC has criteria for membership which normally require applicants to have a high academic standard in a relevant subject, as well as practical ability, an understanding of theory and a scientific approach to treating behavioural problems. The APBC became involved in discussions with Southampton University's Anthrozoology Institute about the need for the creation of a course to provide those possessing the right credentials with the opportunity to acquire a recognised qualification. The University went on to develop a post-graduate course in pet behaviour counselling. This has now been upgraded to a diploma and MSc.

This course provides the necessary theoretical knowledge regarding the treatment of problem behaviours, that is necessary to complement the practical abilities required of a pet behaviour counsellor. Other relevant courses are now also run at Edinburgh, De Montfort and Anglia Universities. From the spring of 1998 the APBC will be providing a more practical course for those with the necessary academic qualifications to provide further insight into the application of the theory where it is necessary.

Finding Further Help

Please ask your vet to refer you to a pet behaviour counsellor such as a member of the APBC, if you cannot find your dog's behaviour problem in this book, or feel that the problems your are experiencing with your dog are severe, or want to be sure that you have identified what the problem is correctly. The solutions outlined in this book are only guidelines to treating behaviour problems, and you should seek profes-sional advice if you feel you need further help or personal guidance.

Contacting the APBC

If you need help with your pet's behaviour and want to know the location of your nearest APBC member, please send an A5 stamped addressed envelope to: APBC, PO Box 46, Worcester, WR8 9YS, England Tel + Fax: +44 (0) 1386 751151
E mail: apbc@petbcent.demon.co.uk
Or you can find information about the APBC on the world wide web

at: http://www.apbc.org.uk

The APBC can also provide a booklist for further reading.

APBC Overseas

The APBC have members in most European countries, North America, Australia and New Zealand. Please contact the UK office for further details.

The Pet Behaviour Centre

The Pet Behaviour Centre in Worcestershire is the main office of David Appleby's behaviour practice. As well as consulting there, he runs monthly clinics at the Queens Veterinary School, Cambridge, and at veterinary centres in Derby, Nottingham, Northampton and Birmingham, and at the RSPCA centre in Leicester. Practice associates run clinics in North Devon, King's Lynn, Bristol, Oxford, Ipswich, Norwich, N.W. London and Thrapston (equine only).

Puppy socialisation classes and bereavement counselling are provided by an Associate in the Coventry area.

For further details, please contact The Pet Behaviour Centre tel: **01386 750615** (fax 750743)

email: Mailroom@petbcent.demon.co.uk.

More details are available on the World Wide Web at

http://www.petbcent.demon.co.uk.

Items of equipment described in this book are also available from the Pet Behaviour Centre: house lines, long lines, training discs, clickers, double-ended leads.

The Association of Pet Dog Trainers (APDT)

You can contact the APDT by writing to: APDT, Peacocks Farm, North Chapel, Petworth, W. Sussex GU28 9JB

More details are available on the World Wide Web at:

(http://www.k9netuk.com/apdt.)

Index